Jagdgeschwader 27 'Afrika'

Aviation Elite Units • 12

Jagdgeschwader 27
'Afrika'

John Weal
Series editor Tony Holmes

Front cover

On the afternoon of 7 August 1942, four Bf 109s of II./JG 27 lifted off from the *Gruppe's* base at Quotaifiya, on the Mediterranean coast road some 45 miles (72 km) west of El Alamein, for a routine *freie Jagd* ('free-hunting') patrol behind Allied lines. At the same time a solitary Bristol Bombay transport aircraft of No 216 Sqn was making the daily flight from Heliopolis to the frontlines in Egypt to pick up wounded soldiers and fly them back to hospitals in the Cairo area. At the forward landing strip at Burg-el-Arab, Sgt H G James, the 18-year-old pilot of the Bombay, was ordered to wait for a special passenger. This proved to Lt Gen William Gott, who just hours earlier had been appointed commander of the 8th Army, and now required transport back to Cairo for an urgent meeting to discuss his future responsibilities.

The Bombay flights were usually made at low level – some 50 ft (15 metres) off the desert – to avoid the unwelcome attention of Luftwaffe fighters. However, on this occasion an overheating Bristol Pegasus XXII engine forced Sgt James to seek cooler air at 500 ft (150 metres). It was at this altitude that the lumbering transport was spotted south south-east of Alexandria by the *Schwarm* of Bf 109s, led by Oberfeldwebel Emil Clade, patrolling high above.

Armed with only two Vickers machine guns, the Bombay was no match for the four fighters of 5./JG 27 swooping down on it like hawks from 20,000 ft (6000 metres). At Clade's first burst of fire James attempted a forced landing, and as passengers and crew began to scramble from the still-moving machine, Unteroffizier Bernhard Schneider carried out a strafing run, killing all but one of those still inside. Among the 17 dead was Lt Gen Gott (whose nickname among the troops was, ironically, 'Strafer'), the highest ranking British soldier to be killed by enemy fire in World War 2.

The Bombay was the sole victim of this particular *freie Jagd* sweep, but this single kill had far-reaching consequences. The loss of Gott meant that a new commander had to be found for the 8th Army, and the officer chosen was the little-known Bernard Law Montgomery. He it was

First published in Great Britain in 2003 by Osprey Publishing
Elms Court, Chapel Way, Botley, Oxford, OX2 9LP

ISBN 1 84176 538 4

Edited by Tony Holmes
Page design by Mark Holt
Cover Artwork by Mark Postlethwaite
Aircraft Profiles by John Weal
Index by Alan Thatcher
Origination by Grasmere Digital Imaging, Leeds, UK
Printed by Stamford Press Pte Ltd, Singapore

03 04 05 06 07   10 9 8 7 6 5 4 3 2 1

ACKNOWLEDGEMENTS
The author would like to thank the following individuals for their generous help in providing information and photographs.
In England – Roger A Freeman, Michael Payne, Dr Alfred Price, Jerry Scutts, Robert Simpson, Andy Thomas and W J A 'Tony' Wood.
In Germany – Herren Georg Clemens, Manfred Griehl, Walter Matthiesen, Paul Schäfer and Harald Weber.

EDITORS NOTE
To make this series as authoritative as possible, the Editor would be interested in hearing from any individual who may have relevant photographs, documentation or first-hand experiences relating to the world's elite combat units, their pilots and aircraft, of the various theatres of war. Any material used will be credited to its original source. Please write to Tony Holmes at 10 Prospect Road, Sevenoaks, Kent, TN13 3UA, Great Britain, or by e-mail at: tony.holmes@osprey-jets.freeserve.co.uk

For details of all Osprey Publishing titles please contact us at:

Osprey Direct UK, P.O. Box 140, Wellingborough, Northants NN8 2FA, UK
E-mail: info@ospreydirect.co.uk

Osprey Direct USA c/o MBI Publishing, P.O. Box 1, 729 Prospect Ave, Osceola, WI 54020, USA
E-mail: info@ospreydirectusa.com

Or visit our website: www.ospreypublishing.com

who led the Allies to victory in the historic Battle of El Alamein two months later, and who – risen to the rank of field marshal – accepted the final surrender of all German forces in north-west Europe on 4 May 1945 (*cover artwork by Mark Postlethwaite*)

CONTENTS

CHAPTER ONE
ORIGINS AND *SITZKRIEG* 6

CHAPTER TWO
BATTLES OF FRANCE AND BRITAIN 18

CHAPTER THREE
MARITA AND *BARBAROSSA* 41

CHAPTER FOUR
AFRICA – THE 'FINEST HOUR' 64

CHAPTER FIVE
THE MEDITERRANEAN, AEGEAN AND BALKANS 90

CHAPTER SIX
THE FINAL BATTLES 103

APPENDICES 121
COLOUR PLATES COMMENTARY 123

INDEX 128

ORIGINS AND *SITZKRIEG*

In the history of aerial warfare, few units are as indelibly linked with the name of one man and with one theatre of operations as is JG 27 with Hans-Joachim Marseille and the Western Desert. Yet this unlikely, although admittedly explosive, combination of a jazz-loving young Berliner and the arid wastes of North Africa lasted a scant 17 months. It thus accounts for just one quarter of the *Geschwader's* overall wartime career – a career which spanned the entire conflict from the first day of hostilities until the last, and which saw the unit's Bf 109s represented on every major fighting front, with the sole exception of Scandinavia, contested by the *Jagdwaffe*.

Although, strictly speaking, *Jagdgeschwader* 27 was a wartime creation, its roots can be traced back to the spring of 1937. This was the period of greatest expansion within the pre-war Luftwaffe, and resulted in the doubling of its existing strength. As far as the fighter arm was concerned, it meant increasing the number of *Jagdgruppen* from six to twelve (plus the activation of a further twelve initially autonomous *Jagdstaffeln*).

The majority of the new *Gruppen* were to be formed by the so-called *Mutter-Tochterverband* (mother-daughter unit) method. This entailed detaching a cadre of experienced personnel – sometimes a whole *Staffel* – from an existing *Gruppe* and using it as the nucleus around which to create a completely new formation. One of the *Jagdgruppen* selected to play the part of a 'mother' unit in the expansion programme of spring 1937 was II./JG 132 'Richthofen', then based at Jüterbog-Damm to the south of Berlin. And the new *Gruppe* it was instrumental in bringing into being was to be designated I./JG 131.

As the final digit of its three-figure designation indicates, I./JG 131 was scheduled to come under the control of *Luftkreiskommando* I. At that time Germany was divided into seven of these 'territorial air commands', with *Luftkreis* I being the command covering all of East Prussia. This eastern-most German province was physically cut off from the rest of the Reich by the intervening Polish 'corridor', a strip of land which afforded the Poles their only access to the Baltic Sea.

On 15 March 1937 Hauptmann Bernhard Woldenga was appointed *Kommandeur* of the as-yet incomplete *Gruppe*. The 36-year-old Woldenga, a former merchant marine officer with he Hamburg-Amerika Line, had transferred his allegiance to maritime aviation in 1929. Serving first with the Reichsmarine, and then the Luftwaffe, he had spent the last year as *Staffelkapitän* of 6./JG 134.

Towards the end of March the *Gruppe's* complement of aircraft, at first comprising a mix of obsolescent Ar 65s and He 50s, began to fly in to East Prussia. Although a stretch of railway track (once part of the busy Berlin-Königsberg main line) connected the isolated territory of East Prussia to the

The 35-year-old ex-merchant marine officer Hauptmann Bernhard Woldenga – pictured here later in the war as an Oberstleutnant – was entrusted with forming I./JG 131 in the spring of 1937

Reich proper, all the *Gruppe*'s heavy equipment and stores were shipped in by sea along the Baltic coast. This was deemed more advisable than subjecting wagon loads of military freight to scrutiny by Polish border guards at either end of the 70-mile (115 km) rail route across the 'corridor'.

I./JG 131 was officially activated on 1 April 1937. The *Gruppe* took up residence at Jesau, a new airfield situated some 14 miles (22 km) south south-east of the provincial capital Königsberg. Despite an 'undeniable sense of separation' from the main body of the Luftwaffe (the only other flying units on permanent station in East Prussia at this time were a couple of reconnaissance *Gruppen*), Woldenga was determined that I./JG 131 would be the equal of – if not better than – 'any home-based *Jagdgruppe*'.

Ably assisted by his three *Staffelkapitäne*, Woldenga set about bringing I./JG 131 up to a peak of operational efficiency. His task was made that much easier when, after just six months, the ageing Ar 65s and He 50s were replaced by more modern Arado Ar 68Fs. These elegant pale-grey biplanes were soon resplendent in the *Gruppe*'s gloss-black trim, which showed up their new white tactical markings to perfection.

A Luftwaffe directive of September 1936 had allowed the fighter arm to dispense with the cumbersome five-digit alphanumeric code system which was the standard marking then worn by all operational aircraft. In its place, the *Jagdwaffe* was allocated a simplified combination of white numbers and geometric symbols. While these new high-visibility markings did have the desired effect of facilitating rapid air-to-air recognition, they also had one drawback – fighters were now the only operational machines in the Luftwaffe not to carry some form of unit identification.

To solve this problem, from late 1936 until early 1938 – the swansong years of the biplane fighter in Luftwaffe service – every *Jagdgeschwader*, or part thereof, was given its own individual colour code. This was usually applied to the engine cowling, and often extended back along the fuselage spine. The most famous of these colour codes was perhaps the red trim worn by the He 51s of JG 132 'Richthofen' in honour, it is commonly believed, of the famous 'Red Baron' himself. Other colours in use included green, orange, tan and light blue.

The *Gruppe's* Ar 68F fighters wore distinctive black trim. Aircraft of 1. *Staffel* carried no other distinguishing unit markings, whereas those of 2. *Staffel*, as here, featured a white band around the nose and rear fuselage (the latter just visible on 'White 9', the third machine in this line-up)

3. *Staffel* was identified by a white disc on the nose and aft fuselage. The efficacy of this simple air-to-air recognition system is well illustrated by this tidy *Kette* of 3./JG 131 machines patrolling the skies of East Prussia

And whereas the 'SA Brownshirt' tan trim applied to JG 134's Ar 68s was an overtly political statement – as was the unit's name, 'Horst Wessel', in commemoration of a much-lauded Nazi 'martyr' – the choice of black for JG 131, as far as is known, in no way implied any association or affiliation with the black-uniformed members of Himmler's notorious SS.

At the end of October 1937, just as the Ar 68Fs were coming into service, Hauptmann Woldenga lost his most experienced *Staffelkapitän* when 3./JG 131's Oberleutnant Eberhard von Trützschler-d'Elsa – who, like the *Kommandeur* himself had received his fighter training at the Luftwaffe's secret Lipezk establishment in the Soviet Union – departed for Spain to command the *Legion Condor's* 4.J/88. Woldenga was fortunate in that d'Elsa's replacement was of equally high calibre. Oberleutnant Max Dobislav would later rise to become *Gruppenkommandeur* of III./JG 27.

In the event, the Ar 68Fs lasted little longer than the original complement of Ar 65s and He 50s, for in May 1938 the *Gruppe* was scheduled to begin re-equipment with the Bf 109. Selected pilots were ordered back to the Reich where their new mounts – a somewhat motley assortment of Bf 109Bs, Cs and Ds – awaited collection at a Luftwaffe depot.

With military aircraft forbidden to overfly the Polish corridor, the return flight to East Prussia involved a dogleg course out over the Baltic, with each pilot being careful to recognise the international three-mile (5-km) limit. Unknown to them, however, the Poles had unilaterally declared a six-mile (10-km) exclusion zone, and their coastal anti-aircraft batteries opened fire on several of the passing Bf 109s! For the *Gruppe*, it was an unexpected and unwelcome baptism of fire, which fortunately caused no damage.

Looking purposeful and warlike in its dark green camouflage, the advent of the Bf 109 heralded the end of the fighter arm's short-lived colourful unit identity trim. For the remaining seven years of its existence, the *Jagdwaffe* would lack any form of standard marking system which would allow an individual fighter's parent unit to be identified (although those *Jagdgeschwader* which later flew as part of the Defence of the Reich organisation did revert to a style of colour coding with their distinctive aft fuselage bands).

The only way a Luftwaffe fighter could disclose its identity was by wearing a unit badge. But such emblems were not compulsory. Their display, or otherwise, was entirely at the discretion of the commanding officer. And whereas badges of all shapes, sizes and subjects proliferated during the pre- and early war years, they gradually became less common as hostilities continued (on the eastern front they were officially banned early in 1943 in an attempt to deny intelligence to the enemy).

Bernhard Woldenga lost little time in devising a *Gruppe* badge for his new Bf 109s. Although of Friesian (North Sea coastal) descent himself, he was greatly impressed by the influence exerted by the Teutonic knights of old on the Baltic territories, which included the very area over which I./JG 131 was now operating. Consequently, he chose their ancient symbol of the Crusaders' Cross, black on a white shield, and brought it up to date by superimposing three small Bf 109 silhouettes in yellow.

If the pilots of the *Gruppe* needed any proof of the increasing political tension in Europe in 1938, the itchy trigger fingers of the Polish anti-aircraft gunners had provided it. Isolated in their East Prussian enclave, I./JG 131 had played no part in Hitler's annexation of Austria in March. But when the Führer upped the pressure later in the year by demanding that the Sudeten regions of Czechoslovakia be ceded to the Greater German Reich, it led to the *Gruppe*'s only operational foray beyond the borders of its home province prior to the outbreak of World War 2.

Early in August 1938, as part of the build-up of military forces being amassed close to the Czech frontier, 2. and 3./JG 131 were transferred south to Liegnitz, in Silesia (no doubt giving the 'corridor' a wide berth en route!), to add their strength to the fighter patrol activity being mounted along the disputed zone.

Hitler's blatant display of military muscle, which ultimately included some 12 Luftwaffe bomber and fighter *Geschwader*, had the desired effect. Deciding that a policy of appeasement was their only option, the British and French governments signed the Munich Agreement, delivering the Sudetenland into the hands of a grateful Führer on 1 October 1938.

Nine days later, the Bf 109s of I./JG 131 moved some 110 miles (160 km) further south into the newly acquired territory, taking up residence at Mährisch-Trübau (Moravska Trebova), a base recently vacated by the Czech Air Force. Their stay was to be of short duration. By the third week of October the *Gruppe* was back at Jesau. Here, a change of designation awaited them.

On 1 August 1938 *Luftkreis* 1 (ex-I), the area command which controlled all of East Prussia, had been replaced by *Luftwaffenkommando Ostpreussen* (AF Command East Prussia). This was but part of a major reorganisation at higher command levels, which had seen the dissolution of the seven original *Luftkreise* and the activation of three larger *Luftwaffengruppenkommandos* (AF Group Commands) in their stead.

The disappearance of the *Luftkreise* had rendered meaningless the final figure of the flying units' three-digit designations. The necessary changes had been postponed, however, to avoid complications during the period of the Sudeten crisis. But on 1 November wholesale redesignations took place. All units coming under the control of *Lw.Gp.Kdo. 1* (HQ Berlin) were given the number '1' as the third digit of their designator. Thus the 'Richthofen' *Geschwader* based in the Berlin area (hitherto JG 132) now became JG 131, while Bernhard Woldenga's 'original' I./JG 131 – part of the semi-autonomous *Lw.Kdo. Ostpreussen* – suddenly found itself operating as I./JG 130.

But this method of nomenclature was still clumsy, and on 1 May 1939 one last effort was made to simplify command titles and unit designations. The *Luftwaffengruppenkommandos* (now numbering four) were renamed *Luftflotten* (Air Fleets), and the flying units controlled by each air fleet were renumbered in sequential blocks of 25 (thus *Luftflotte* 1's units fell within block 1 to 25, with *Luftflotte* 2 being allocated 26 to 50, and so on).

At the same time *Lw.Kdo Ostpreussen* was incorporated into *Luftflotte* 1. For some reason Woldenga's obscure and little-known Jesau-based *Gruppe* was given numerical pride of place within the new system. They now emerged as I./JG 1, leaving the Luftwaffe's premier fighter unit, the highly-publicised *Jagdgeschwader* 'Richthofen', in decidedly second place as JG 2.

Little more than a month after assuming their new identity, I./JG 1 began re-equipping with the Bf 109E. And a month later still, in mid-July 1939, it was their turn to play the part of a 'mother' unit in the final emergency expansion programme implemented just before the commencement of hostilities.

Having recently completed conversion on to the Bf 109E, I./JG 1 was able not only to provide a cadre of experienced personnel for the *Gruppe* being formed, but was also in a position to furnish it with a full complement of their 'cast-off' Bf 109Ds. Designated I./JG 21, the new unit spent the first few days of its existence alongside I./JG 1 at Jesau, before moving to Gutenfeld, some ten miles (16 km) closer to Königsberg, on 24 July. Perhaps to cement the 'mother-daughter' relationship between the two *Gruppen*, I./JG 21's *Kommandeur*, Major Martin Mettig, opted for a unit badge very similar to that of I./JG 1, but in different colours (see *Osprey Aviation Elite 6 - Jagdgeschwader 54 'Grünherz'*).

The concessions made at the time of the Munich Agreement may have appeased Hitler temporarily, but they had far from satisfied his craving for further territorial expansion. In March 1939 he had gained control of the rest of Czechoslovakia. Now he had his sights on Poland, and this time he was determined to use force of arms. During August all three branches of the Wehrmacht began to position their units in readiness for the coming confrontation with the Poles.

The advent of the Bf 109 ushered in a new era of anonymity for Luftwaffe fighters. Basking in the midday sun at Jesau in the early summer of 1939, Hauptmann Woldenga's Bf 109E identifies itself only by the *Gruppe* badge below the windscreen. The white disc on the rear of the fuselage is believed to be a temporary war-games marking. And with the canopy open and starting-handle in place (projecting from the engine cowling ahead of the badge), the next practice scramble cannot be far off

Groundcrew of I./JG 1 (as the *Gruppe* became on 1 May 1939) display a large-scale replica of the unit badge designed by Bernhard Woldenga and based upon the Crusaders' Cross shield of the Teutonic Knights

By mid-August 1939 the time for practising was over. Deployed at Seerappen, these machines of the *Gruppenstab*, with the Adjutant's in the foreground, are very much on a war footing as hostilities with Poland are only a matter of days away

The accepted Luftwaffe policy of the period was that the Bf 109 units would be retained on home soil for purely defensive purposes, leaving the new, twin-engined Bf 110 *Zerstörer* – on which great hopes were being pinned – to undertake offensive missions in the field and carry the fight to the enemy.

Consequently, in mid-August 1939, Hauptmann Woldenga was ordered to vacate Jesau and deploy his three *Staffeln* slightly further to the south in a defensive line stretching across the width of East Prussia, from Heiligenbeil, close to the Baltic coast, via Schippenbeil in the centre, to Arys-Rostken, which was only some 18 miles (30 km) from the Polish frontier.

It was from these three fields that I./JG 1's 46 Bf 109Es awaited the Polish response to the German invasion, launched in the early hours of 1 September. But the expected enemy counter-attacks failed to materialise, and the Polish air force made few incursions into East Prussian airspace. Its aircraft were almost wholly committed in combating the Wehrmacht's armoured spearheads which, within a matter of hours, were already biting deep into Poland. When Polish bomber crews pleaded for permission to bomb Königsberg on the third day of hostilities, their superiors' denial of the request reportedly brought them 'very near to mutiny'!

The *Gruppe*'s part in, and impact upon, the Polish campaign was therefore minimal. It made no claims for enemy aircraft destroyed, and its only casualty was a 2. *Staffel* pilot slightly wounded by 'friendly' flak. Its participation was also to be short-lived. After brief deployment to more forward fields closer to the border with Poland, and to one just across the frontier in newly-occupied enemy territory, I./JG 1 began to move back to Jesau on 5 September.

Its defensive capabilities may not have been stretched when it came to the protection of East Prussia, but the declaration of war against Germany

by Great Britain and France on 3 September 1939 obviously posed a potentially far greater aerial threat to the Reich – at least in the minds of the Luftwaffe High Command (Ob.d.L.) back in Berlin. For hardly had the now Major Woldenga's three *Staffeln* returned to Jesau before orders were received transferring them to north-west Germany.

By the late summer of 1939 the Luftwaffe's preparations and readiness for war were nowhere near as advanced as the Western Allies had been led to believe. Skilful German propaganda had portrayed the air arm of the Third Reich as an all-powerful force. The reality was somewhat different. *Luftflotte* 2, for example, the air fleet which controlled all operational flying units in the north-west quadrant of Germany – a vast area fronted by land and sea borders together stretching some 620 miles (1000 km) in length – had just one resident *Jagdgeschwader* (JG 26).

Upon the outbreak of hostilities steps were quickly taken to increase the Luftwaffe's fighter presence in north-western Germany. On 21 September an order marked 'Most Urgent' was issued by the Braunschweig (Brunswick) HQ of *Luftflotte* 2. This called for the immediate activation of a second *Jagdgeschwader*, which was to be based at Neumünster in Schleswig-Holstein.

In the event, and before mobilisation of the *Geschwaderstab* was even fully completed, countermanding instructions arrived from the Ob.d.L. directing that the skeleton organisation – already officially referred to as JG 27 – was to be renumbered as *Stab* JG 77.

Ten days later a totally fresh start was made with the cutting of a second set of orders. And on 1 October 1939 both the *Geschwaderstab* and the I. *Gruppe* of a new *Jagdgeschwader* 27 were formally activated at Münster-Handorf.

The man chosen to be JG 27's first *Kommodore* was Oberstleutnant Max Ibel. Born in 1896, Ibel had volunteered for military service in World War 1, seeing action on the Somme as an officer with a Bavarian sapper battalion, before transferring to the special flamethrower detachment of a guards regiment (Garde Res.Pi.Rgt.1). He too was a later alumnus of the secret Lipezk training establishment in the USSR, an experience which no doubt stood him in good stead when, in 1934, he was tasked with setting up the Luftwaffe's first fighter pilots' school at Schleissheim. Prior to assuming command of JG 27, Oberstleutnant Ibel had been serving as *Kommodore* of JG 3.

Sharing the Handorf base on the north-eastern outskirts of Münster with Ibel's *Stab* was his sole *Gruppe*, I./JG 27. This was placed in the capable hands of Hauptmann Helmut Riegel, who had previously been a member of staff of the air warfare academy at Werder/Havel.

Another indication of the Luftwaffe's unpreparedness for war was the relatively large number of individual *Jagdgruppen* (and *Jagdstaffel*) which had been activated, but which did not yet have a parent *Geschwaderstab* and were still operating on a semi-autonomous basis. Once war had been declared an attempt was made to introduce some measure of uniformity into the *Jagdwaffe*'s order of battle by apportioning these hitherto 'orphan' *Gruppen* among the existing *Jagdgeschwaderstäbe* – not one of which, incidentally, had yet been raised to full three-*Gruppe* establishment!

Ibel's *Stab* JG 27, with its single component *Gruppe*, was an obvious candidate for such an infusion of outside strength, and the two *Jagdgrup-*

The first *Kommodore* of JG 27 was 43-year-old Oberstleutnant Max Ibel, a veteran of the trenches of World War 1. He is seen here, second from the right, after promotion to Oberst – and wearing the Knight's Cross awarded at the height of the Battle of Britain – in somewhat earnest discussion with members of his staff. *Brigadegeneral* (retd) Max Ibel died in March 1981, aged 85

pen now assigned to his command were the pair previously stationed in far-off East Prussia, I./JG 1 and I./JG 21.

After a ten-day stop-over at Lübeck-Blankensee, the Bf 109Es of Major Woldenga's I./JG 1 had flown in to Vörden, north of Osnabrück, by 15 September. I./JG 21's Bf 109Ds, led by Major Martin Mettig, arrived at Plantlünne, close to the Dortmund-Ems canal, a month later. This meant that by mid-October, the three *Gruppen* of Oberstleutnant Ibel's *'Geschwader'* were ranged in a tight defensive arc, the border with neutral Holland in front of them and the flat expanse of the north German hinterland at their backs.

Although this sector of the western front did not witness the periodic fighter skirmishes which flared up during the autumn months along Germany's common frontier with France further to the south, it did experience the occasional RAF reconnaissance intruder. These were usually Blenheim bombers, whose crews displayed a punctilious regard for Dutch neutrality by either approaching from across the North Sea or, less frequently, by circumnavigating the southernmost tip of neutral Luxembourg.

The first of these had already fallen victim to I./JG 1 within a fortnight of the *Gruppe's* arrival at Vörden. On 28 September Feldwebel Klaus Faber of 3./JG 1 had shot down a Blenheim IV of UK-based No 110 Sqn that had been sent to reconnoitre the Osnabrück area. Seventy-two hours later, on 1 October (the day the *Gruppe* was placed under the command of *Stab* JG 27), Oberleutnant Walter Adolph, the *Staffelkapitän* of 2./JG 1, claimed a second Blenheim IV (of No 139 Sqn, also stationed in England) which he brought down east of Paderborn.

Before the month was out two further Blenheims, both French-based Mk Is, would be credited to the ex-East Prussian *Gruppen*. On 16 October 3./JG 1's Leutnant Hans-Volkert Rosenboom destroyed a No 57 Sqn machine attempting a reconnaissance of the Wesel-Bocholt railway.

A reporter sought out Rosenboom, and his description of the action appeared in several local newspapers two days later. After recounting how he had taken off to pursue the intruder, which passed overhead at an altitude of some 3000 m (10,000 ft), Rosenboom explained that the enemy machine tried to escape by diving into a cloud bank;

'I dived even more steeply, and as I came out of the layer of cloud I saw him emerge from the cloud above me. He immediately dived lower still, and there then began a wild pursuit which almost defies description. The *Engländer* was a very capable, clever and resourceful pilot. He made use of every undulation in the terrain, every hedge, every ditch, every building as cover. He dodged between trees. Close on his tail, I could see smashed treetops silhouetted against the sky and bits of foliage flying through the air (in fact, the British pilot had momentarily misjudged his height, and clipping the treetops had smashed the perspex nose of the Blenheim and caused the port engine to stall).

'I half expected him to take one or two rooftops with him, for at times we were both only some two metres (six feet) above the ground. But whenever he had to gain a little height to clear an obstruction, I sent another burst into his crate (one of the Blenheim's crew likened this to the noise of 'someone shaking rusty nails in a metal can!').

'Escape was out of the question', Rosenboom concluded his account, 'at last, one final volley, and I saw the pilot put his machine down on its belly in a potato field. All three occupants jumped out as the smoking Blenheim burst into flames.'

Exactly two weeks later it was I./JG 21's turn to score when Leutnant Heinz Lange brought down a Blenheim of No 18 Sqn near Meppen. As with the other three pilots mentioned above, it was the first kill for future Knight's Cross recipient Lange, who would end the war as *Kommodore* of JG 51 'Mölders'.

This quartet of hapless Blenheims would prove to be the only victories achieved by Ibel's units during the opening eight months of hostilities (the period of relative inactivity which has since come to be known as the 'Phoney War' or *Sitzkrieg*). The rapidly worsening weather conditions – the winter of 1939/40 was the harshest the region had known for many years – soon began to have a noticeable effect, both on the scale of operations and on serviceability figures.

The coming months were therefore marked instead by a higher than usual proportion of accidents, four of them fatal, and a succession of temporary deployments to other fields within JG 27's area of control.

In the very depths of the winter, between November 1939 and January 1940, Oberstleutnant Ibel's command was temporarily enlarged by the addition of two further *Gruppen*. I.(J)/LG 2, originally part of a trials and evaluation unit, but now serving as a standard *Jagdgruppe* flying BF 109Es, took up short-term residence on several airfields near Cologne, including Gymnich and Butzweilerhof. *Jagdgruppe* 126, which was the current *nom de guerre* of III./ZG 26, a *Zerstörer* unit still awaiting delivery of its Bf 110s, and having to operate Bf 109Ds in the interim, occupied first Bönninghardt and then Lippstadt. Neither *Gruppe* achieved any victories or suffered any known losses during their brief periods of secondment to JG 27.

In February 1940 – by which time *Stab*, I./JG 27 and I./JG 1 were congregated at Krefeld, with I./JG 21 at nearby München-Gladbach – several changes of command took place. Both the ex-East Prussian *Gruppen* lost their long-serving *Kommandeure*. I./JG 21's Major Mettig departed to head the newly activated *Geschwaderstab* JG 54, and his place was in turn taken by Hauptmann Fritz Ultsch, previously the *Staffelkapitän* of 1./JG 77. Major Bernhard Woldenga of I./JG 1 was promoted to a staff position in the office of Inspectorate of Fighters. He in turn was replaced by Hauptmann Joachim Schlichting, the erstwhile *Geschwader*-Adjutant of JG 27.

This meant that Oberstleutnant Ibel required the services of a new adjutant. The officer who arrived to fill this position was a certain Hauptmann Adolf Galland. A passionate fighter pilot, Galland had served with the *Legion Condor* in Spain. There, however, he had been appointed *Staffelkapitän* of 3.(J)/88. This was not at all to his liking, for while the *Legion*'s other fighter units were busy converting on to the Bf 109, 3. *Staffel* had been ordered to retain their Heinkel He 51s (an obsolescent biplane type that was by then completely outclassed by contemporary Republican fighter opposition) for use in support of the Nationalist ground armies.

By early 1940 JG 27's fighters were beginning to appear in the new *hellblau* 'air superiority' finish. This particular machine, flown by the *Gruppenkommandeur* of I./JG 27, Hauptmann Helmut Riegel, who would also fall victim to RAF fighters during the Battle of Britain, still displays the small, pre-war style fuselage cross, which perhaps suggests that it previously wore dark-green camouflage before being re-painted in the new scheme

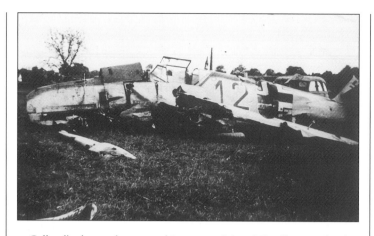

With a standard *Balkenkreuz* and even higher camouflage demarcation line than the aircraft seen on page 15, this aircraft of 2./JG 27 is more likely to have been a recent delivery factory-finished in *hellblau*. One of a number of accidents suffered by Max Ibel's *Gruppen* during the opening months of 1940, the events leading up to 'Red 12's' present sorry state are not known – let's hope the wine bottle perched precariously on the aft cockpit glazing just in front of the aerial mast had nothing to do with it!

Galland's thoroughness was his own undoing. His efforts to develop and perfect a whole new set of low-level attack and ground-support tactics were to prove so successful that when he returned from Spain he was not permitted to rejoin the fighter arm. Instead, now an acknowledged 'ground-attack expert', he was posted to the Luftwaffe's sole assault *Gruppe* – Hs 123-equipped II.(Schl)/LG 2.

As *Kapitän* of this unit's 5. *Staffel*, he had flown close-support missions during the campaign in Poland. But enough was enough! Galland sought the connivance of a friendly doctor to have himself pronounced unfit for further flying in an open cockpit. Armed with this medical 'evidence', the way was at last clear for his return to the fighter fraternity. Hauptmann Adolf Galland's appointment as *Geschwader*-Adjutant of JG 27 put him firmly back on the rungs of the ladder which would take him to the very pinnacle of his chosen career as the Luftwaffe's *'General der Jagdflieger'*.

By February 1940 a second *Gruppe* had finally been added to JG 27's official table of establishment. But it would be several months before II./JG 27 actually came under Oberstleutnant Ibel's direct control.

Formed in the first week of January at Magdeburg-Est under the temporary leadership of Hauptmann Erich von Selle, the *Gruppe* transferred to Döberitz, on the western outskirts of Berlin, in mid-February. Commanded now by Hauptmann Werner Andres (ex-*Staffelkapitän* of 1./JG 3), here it would remain – except for two brief deployments to

A trio of I./JG 1's *Emils* being serviced outside a tented hangar at Gymnich in May 1940, immediately prior to the *Blitzkrieg* in the west. Close examination reveals that the machine on the far left is still wearing the large full-chord underwing crosses (extending over the landing flaps) which were introduced as a result of the ground-to-air recognition problems experienced in Poland

Bönninghardt and Essen – forming part of the aerial defence of the German capital until the spring.

During this period II./JG 27 was subordinated first to JG 3 and then to JG 51. And it was under the latter *Stab* that the *Gruppe* returned to the western front early in May – 4. and 6. *Staffel*n to Wesel, 5. *Staffel* to Bönninghardt – this time in earnest, as German forces began gathering for the invasion of France and the Low Countries.

In the meantime, Oberstleutnant Ibel's *'Geschwader'* had also taken station on the fields which were to be its jumping-off points for the planned *Blitzkrieg* in the west. *Stab* and I./JG 27 had joined I./JG 21 at München-Gladbach, while I./JG 1 were quartered some 28 miles (45 km) away at Gymnich, to the south-west of Cologne.

It was at München-Gladbach on 9 April 1940 that General Wolfram *Frhr.* von Richthofen presented I./JG 27 with its *Gruppe* standard. After the ceremonial parade, which had included these telling words from von Richthofen, 'Fulfilment of duty does not imply the achievement of one's own personal aims, but means serving the common good', orders were given that the standard was to be flown at the start of every operational mission.

Thus the stage was set for JG 27's real baptism of fire.

Just before the invasion of France I./JG 27 began sporting their prescient, and now famous, '*Afrika*' badge, which was a continuation of the colonial theme first introduced by 2. *Staffel* (see colour profile 6). Note that these are machines of the *Gruppenstab* pictured at Plumetot during the Battle of Britain

BATTLES OF FRANCE AND BRITAIN

The invasion of the west in the spring of 1940 was to be a re-run of the *Blitzkrieg* tactics which had demolished the bulk of Poland's armed forces in just 18 days the previous autumn.

One of the most important components of the *Blitzkrieg* armoury employed against the Poles had been Generalmajor von Richthofen's *Fliegerführer z.b.V.*, a special air command composed mainly of Ju 87B dive-bombers. Since augmented by a *Kampfgeschwader* of Do 17Z twin-engined bombers and upgraded to the status of a *Fliegerkorps*, von Richthofen's 'flying artillery' formed the hammer which would be used to breach the chain of formidable frontier defences protecting the borders of neutral Belgium and Holland along the northernmost flank of the forthcoming invasion.

Recognising that fighter opposition in the west would pose a far greater danger to his pilots than that faced in Poland, von Richthofen's command was now also assigned its own protective fighter force. This was the task entrusted to Oberstleutnant Ibel's three subordinate *Gruppen*. But first they had another, and perhaps even more vital, part to play in the opening hours of *'Fall Gelb'* ('Case Yellow'), the initial phase of the attack against the Low Countries and France.

By the time of the *Blitzkrieg* in the west I./JG 1 had also revised its markings, moving both staff symbols and individual aircraft numerals from the fuselage to the engine cowling. This unique practice is well illustrated by these two machines of the *Gruppenstab* parked under the trees at Gymnich during the first days of the campaign. Once again the starting-handles are in place ready for a quick take-off – but now it's for real!

Indicative of the close cooperation between Max Ibel's fighters and Generalmajor von Richthofen's VIII. *Fliegerkorps,* 'White 15' of 1./JG 1 undergoes maintenance in the field alongside the Hs 123s of II.(Schl)/LG 2. This latter, the only dedicated ground-attack *Gruppe* in the Luftwaffe at the time, was the unit in which Adolf Galland had served during the campaign in Poland

At 2155 hrs on the evening of 9 May 1940 a terse order had gone out from *Luftflotte* 2 HQ at Münster – 'Execute 0535 hrs'.

In fact the *Blitzkrieg* in the west, launched on 10 May 1940, was spearheaded by waves of Ju 52/3m transports – some laden with paratroops, others towing gliders – which began crossing the German border north of Aachen at 0510 hrs.

As the vulnerable tri-motored transports droned towards their assigned objectives, which included the supposedly impregnable Belgian fort of Eben Emael, linchpin of the northern front defences, they were closely escorted by the Bf 109Es of Max Ibel's JG 27. Once delivered of their lethal burdens, the Ju 52/3ms immediately returned to their bases around Cologne to reload and ferry in fresh troops and supplies. And so it would go throughout the day.

Having covered the early Ju 52/3m missions without undue incident, JG 27's three *Gruppen* turned their attention to their primary role – that of protecting von Richthofen's bombers. These latter did not require the same kind of close-order shepherding which had been provided for the near defenceless Ju 52/3ms. Instead, Ibel's pilots were instructed to gain, and maintain, air superiority over a wide tract of enemy territory to the west of Aachen. This would have the effect of creating an aerial buffer zone, behind which VIII. *Fliegerkorps'* Junkers and Dorniers could operate with relative impunity.

Implementation of these orders led to the first clashes of the campaign for JG 27 and its component *Gruppen*. The first pilot of all to claim a kill on the opening day of the *Blitzkrieg* in the west was Hauptmann Fritz Ultsch, *Gruppenkommandeur* of I./JG 21, who was credited with a Belgian machine (variously cited as a Firefly, Fox or Battle!) shot down over St Trond at 0718 hrs. Some two-and-a-half hours later, just before 1000 hrs, I./JG 27 entered the fray with Unteroffizier Heinrich Becher and Leutnant Erwin Axthelm each claiming a Belgian Gladiator in the Tirlemont area. Later in the morning I./JG 21 went one better by downing a trio of Gladiators over Tongres.

By the day's end the fortress of Eben Emael had been neutralised, vital bridges across the Albert Canal had been seized, and German ground forces were pouring westwards into Belgium and Holland.

On 11 May I./JG 1 opened their *Blitzkrieg* account with the destruction of no fewer than 12 Allied aircraft. Two later luminaries of JG 27, Leutnant Ludwig Franzisket and Unteroffizier Emil Clade, both achieved their first victories on this date. Each got a Gladiator during an early morning mission and went on to add a French MS.406 fighter in mid-evening. But even more successful was Hauptmann Wilhelm Balthasar, *Staffelkapitän* of 1./JG 1, who was credited with three of the seven Belgian Gladiators shot down during the early morning confrontation near Maastricht, and was also responsible for the third of the evening's MS.406s.

In the meantime, two of I./JG 27's future Knight's Cross winners, Oberleutnants Wolfgang Redlich and Gerhard Homuth, currently the *Staffelkapitäne* of 1. and 3./JG 27 respectively, had also claimed their firsts. Redlich's victim was a Battle (probably Belgian) despatched near Tongres at 0740 hrs, while Homuth's Blenheim, shot down south-west of Diest in the late afternoon, was almost certainly a machine of Wattisham-based No 110 Sqn that had been sent to attack the Albert Canal bridges.

The presence of French and Britsh machines in the area was an indication of just how seriously the Allies were taking the threat developing on the northern front. Fearing a repetition of the Schlieffen plan of 1914, which saw the Imperial German Army launch its offensive in the west with a massive right hook through the neutral Low Countries - and nearly capturing Paris as a result – the commanders of 1940 were determined to halt the Wehrmacht at all costs.

The most vulnerable point along the German line of advance was the bottleneck created by the two remaining bridges over the Albert Canal west of Maastricht. If these could be knocked out, the Wehrmacht's progress would be seriously impeded. Allied bombers were ordered to mount an all-out effort. The attacks of 11 May would pale into insignificance against those flown the following day. But by then the Germans, who were equally aware of the vital importance of the Vroenhoven and Veldwezelt bridges, had had a full 48 hours to ring the two structures with flak defences.

Despite the superhuman, almost suicidal, bravery displayed by the RAF bomber crews, the bridges remained intact. The combination of massed batteries of 20 mm and 37 mm anti-aircraft guns, plus the predatory Luftwaffe fighters, wrought havoc among the attackers. By the close of the day's fighting several RAF squadrons had been virtually annihilated.

I./JG 1 claimed ten victories on that 12 May. All were twin-engined Bristol Blenheims, including three for Oberleutnant Walter Adolph, *Staffelkapitän* of 2./JG 1, a brace (downed just two minutes apart) for Leutnant Erbo *Graf* von Kageneck and one for *Gruppenkommandeur* Joachim Schlichting.

I./JG 27's tally was nine. This comprised four Blenheims, an equal number of Hurricanes, and a solitary Fairey Battle. The latter was the only Battle credited to the *Geschwader* on this date. A first for 2. *Staffel*'s Feldwebel Otto Sawallisch, it was, in all likelihood, a machine of No 12 Sqn, whose courageous attack on the bridges against impossible odds was subsequently recognised by the award of the first two (posthumous) air Victoria Crosses of World War 2.

On 12 May 1940 Oberleutnant Gerd Framm, *Staffelkapitän* of 2./JG 27, had opened his score with a hat-trick – two Blenheims and a Hurricane over Maastricht. Pictured here being presented with the Iron Cross, First Class, Framm ended the French campaign as I./JG 27's joint highest scorer, with both he and Oberleutnant Gerhard Homuth (StaKa 3./JG 27) having claimed nine Allied aircraft each

While I./JG 27 and I./JG 1 were thus engaged in and around the immediate environs of the two bridges, I./JG 21 continued to patrol the airspace further to the west. This netted them four Hurricanes near the Belgian capital, Brussels, and a solitary French Curtiss Hawk shot down near Namur.

Even JG 27's *Stabsschwarm* got in on the act, they too being credited with a quartet of Hurricanes. One fell to Leutnant Gustav Rödel, the *Geschwader*-TO (technical officer) close to Huy. The remainder provided the first three aerial victories for the *Legion Condor*'s erstwhile 'ground-attack expert', Hauptmann Adolf Galland;

'Patrolling at 3500 m (12,000 ft) some eight kilometres (five miles) to the west of Liège, we spotted a formation of eight Hurricanes flying 900 m (3000 ft) below us.

'We knew exactly what to do. Having practised for just such a situation countless times over the past few months, our reaction was almost automatic. We went into a dive. The Hurricanes had not yet spotted us. I felt no excitement, nor any of the expected fever of the chase.

'I opened fire from a range which, given the circumstances, was still far too great. But my burst was dead on target. The poor devil finally woke up to what was happening. He attempted a rather clumsy side-slip, which took him straight into the line of fire of my wingman.

'I got him squarely in my sights again, and a second burst sent him spiralling down apparently out of control. I immediately went after another of the now scattered Hurricanes. This one tried to get away by diving. The Belgian did a half-roll and disappeared through a break in the clouds. I stuck to his tail, and this time attacked from very close quarters. He zoomed upwards for a split second, then stalled and dived vertically into the ground from a height of only 450 m (1500 ft).

'During a patrol later that same afternoon I shot down my third Hurricane near Tirlemont.'

From the above account it is clear that Galland believed at the time (and for many years after) that his opponents had been Hurricanes of the Belgian Air Force. In fact, it now seems almost certain that his first two victims were the two machines reported lost in the Liège area by No 87 Sqn RAF. The identity of Galland's third claim is less easy to establish, but again – if it was in fact a Hurricane – it would have been British.

Despite the ferocity of the fighting over Belgium and Holland, these operations on the northern flank were all part of a gigantic feint designed to lure Allied ground forces out of the prepared defence positions in north-east France, which they had been constructing all winter long. The Germans *intended* for them to move forward into open country as they hastened to the aid of the Belgians and Dutch, for the *Blitzkrieg* of 1940 was turning the Schlieffen plan of 1914 on its head.

This time the main thrust of the Wehrmacht's offensive was to come up from the south, spearheaded by the five armoured divisions of the *Panzergruppe* von Kleist which had been assembled, and carefully concealed, in the wooded valleys of the Eifel/Ardennes chain of hills. It was their job to smash through the widening gap opened up between the main bulk of the French Army, still ensconced behind the Maginot Line, and those troops in the north-east – including the British Expeditionary Force (BEF) – ordered forward to the assistance of the Belgians.

But before von Kleist's Panzer columns could fan out across the wide open plains of Artois and Picardy – ideal tank country, which would take them all the way to the Channel coast – they too had a major water obstacle to cross in the River Meuse.

On the afternoon of 13 May the Stukas of VIII. *Fliegerkorps* were ordered to move down closer to the two main crossing points over the Meuse near Sedan and Charleville. They were accompanied by *Stab* and I./JG 27, who flew in to Odendorf, west of Bonn, on that date.

Throughout 14 May even more Allied bombers were sacrificed in a series of attacks trying to halt the German Army at yet another strategically important water barrier. To no avail. By the time darkness fell, nearly 90 of their number – almost equally divided between British and French – had been shot down along the line of the Meuse.

Busy escorting their own Stukas, Ibel's pilots had taken no part in the 'Day of the Fighters', as the 14 May slaughter over the Meuse was to become known in the Luftwaffe. But the subsequent breakout over the twin bridgeheads heralded a new chapter in the history of JG 27. For the first time the Geschwader was experiencing the true meaning of *Blitzkrieg*: not just hard-hitting, but fast-moving as well.

On 16 May VIII. *Fliegerkorps* was instructed to continue its support of the *Panzergruppe* von Kleist all the way to the Channel coast. For the remainder of the month Ibel's three *Gruppen* – augmented since 13 May by the temporary addition of a fourth, I./JG 51 – would be constantly leapfrogging forward in their attempts to keep pace with the armoured spearheads. During this period some units underwent as many as six changes of base, often staying only a matter of hours at some fields.

In spite of the additional difficulties imposed by this war of movement, individual and group scores climbed steadily. Adolf Galland's victim of 16 May, claimed as a Spitfire south of Lille, is now believed to have been a Hurricane of No 85 Sqn. Perhaps more adept at aircraft recognition, pilots of I./JG 27 listed their successes in the Brussels area on this date as four Hurricanes and a Lysander. Four days later their *Gruppenkommandeur*, Hauptmann Helmut Riegel, was credited with his first victory – a French MS.406 fighter north-west of Reims, one of the growing number of *Armée de l'Air* machines which the *Geschwader* would encounter in the days and weeks ahead.

But, inevitably, the increase in activity brought with it casualties. Since moving down to Charleville on 16 May, I./JG 1 had added a further nine enemy aircraft to its scoreboard. Over Amiens on 20 May the unit would get three more – a Potez 63 and a pair of MS.406s. The dogfight with the Moranes was not without cost, however, as 3. *Staffel* lost Leutnant Horst Braxator. He was the *Geschwader's* first combat fatality since the outbreak of war.

Seventy-two hours later I./JG 1 was involved in another fierce clash, this time with Hurricanes east of Arras. The *Gruppe* claimed six of the RAF fighters (three of them falling to Hauptmann Balthasar alone, thereby taking his score into double figures), but suffered a second loss when Unteroffizier Paul Widmer of 2./JG 1 was shot down.

This same 23 May also witnessed the *Geschwader's* first serious encounter with RAF Spitfires. I./JG 27 were credited with three of the UK-based fighters (possibly from No 92 Sqn) over the Dunkirk-Calais area, but only at the cost of four of their own machines. Three pilots survived to become PoWs but the fourth was killed.

By now *Fall Gelb* was approaching its climax. The leading German Panzers had already reached the Channel coast near the mouth of the River Somme, Holland had capitulated, Belgium would soon follow suit, and the BEF was preparing for evacuation.

The first British troops were lifted off the beaches of Dunkirk on 26 May. That day I./JG 1 again escorted Stukas attacking the port of Calais, as Leutnant Erbo *Graf* von Kageneck later recounted;

'We were already strapped into our fighters as the Stukas, heavy with bombs, flew over our forward strip (Monchy-Breton) heading for Calais. Weather conditions were ideal – some lingering early morning mist, the rising sun at our backs and good visibility. We quickly took to the air, got into battle formation as we flew a wide curve, and soon caught up with the Stukas. In several large groups, our fighters gently weaving at either side, we approached the target. It couldn't be missed, even without a compass. A thick column of black smoke showed the way. Shortly before the target the fighters in front warned "Spitfires ahead!" The Spitfire had a very good reputation. Then all hell broke loose.

'Steep climbs, tight turns, stick close together, no way of telling who was friend and who was foe. Break, pull up – there a cloud of smoke, a ball of

By 17 May I./JG 1 had moved forward from Gymnich to Charleville. This large field to the west of Sedan was the first staging-post for many of the Luftwaffe's *Jagdgruppen* as they began the advance through France. Here, 2./JG 1's 'Black 13' is flanked by the burned-out remains of what appear to be *Armée de l'Air* Potez 63.11s, which were presumably the base's previous occupants

fire, a parachute. Then the well known voice of Hauptmann Balthasar over the R/T – *"Abschuss!"*, and somebody immediately confirming the kill with a shout of *'Viktor, Viktor!'"*

In fact, Balthasar got two of the four Spitfires claimed by the *Gruppe* over Calais, but his 1. *Staffel* lost Unteroffizier Rudolf Vogel, whose Bf 109 was shot into the Channel.

JG 21 suffered its first combat fatality that same day when Feldwebel Fridolin Hartwig was brought down over Cambrai during a series of sprawling, mid-morning engagements with large numbers of French fighters further inland. Against this single loss, however, Hauptmann Ultsch's pilots claimed a staggering 22 enemy aircraft!

Stab and I./JG 27 continued to operate over the Dunkirk area throughout the now historic British evacuation. During this period their pilots together claimed a further nine RAF fighters, plus a handful of bombers. Included among the latter was a pair of Wellingtons, possibly of No 37 Sqn, despatched by 2. *Staffel* on the morning of 1 June.

But organisational changes were now afoot as the Luftwaffe began to redeploy its forces for the imminent launch of *Fall Rot* ('Case Red'), the second phase of the attack on France. I./JG 51 had been returned to its parent *Geschwader* on 1 June after having scored some two dozen kills while subordinated to JG 27. And three days later Oberstleutnant Ibel lost the services of his two long-standing ex-East Prussian *Gruppen* when I./JG 1 and I./JG 21 were temporarily detached for service under other *Stäbe*.

To compensate for this sudden loss of 75 per cent of his effective strength Max Ibel was, however, finally able to welcome II. *Gruppe* into the *Geschwader* fold.

II./JG 27 had spent its war in the west to date serving under three different *Stäbe*. Initially attached to JG 51 and responsible for the northernmost flank of the *Blitzkrieg* front, all of the *Gruppe's* first 14 kills (a mix of British and Dutch machines) had been scored over Holland – and mainly around Rotterdam – in the opening 72 hours of the campaign.

These successes had been achieved, at the expense of one Bf 109 lost to anti-aircraft fire, while flying from their bases in Germany, where the *Gruppe* would remain until 18 May. Thereafter, attached first to JG 26

A machine of 5./JG 27, 'Black 3' patrols the northern flank during the opening stages of *Fall Gelb*. On the original (somewhat damaged) print it is just possible to make out that its markings conform to the usual 5. *Staffel* practice of combining the black numeral with a red horizontal *Gruppe* bar (thinly outlined in black) aft of the fuselage cross

and then JG 54, it moved forward into Belgium, becoming engaged primarily in bomber-escort duties. No further claims were made until the last day of the month, when a solitary Lysander was brought down near Dunkirk. Then, on 5 June, II./JG 27 flew in to Guise-North to join its parent *Geschwader*.

JG 27 had been only peripherally involved in Operation *Paula*, the massed bombing raids on military targets in the Greater Paris area mounted on 3 June. But 48 hours later the start of *Fall Rot* saw all three of Ibel's *Gruppen* (I./JG 1 having

returned from its brief detachment to JG 77) heavily committed over the River Somme as the German armies began their push south-westwards into the heart of France.

For the first two days the *Armée de l'Air* fought heroically in support of its own ground troops, who were already showing signs of buckling under the pressure of this renewed offensive. On both 5 and 6 June there were fierce clashes between the opposing sides' fighters. I./JG 27 claimed seven MS.406s to the north of Paris on the first evening of the assault. I./JG 1 had been credited with a round dozen enemy machines – four Moranes, the rest twin-engined bombers – by the close of the day's fighting. In return, each *Gruppe* had lost a single Bf 109, their pilots taken into temporary French captivity.

6 June brought more of the same. I. and II./JG 27 together downed seven French machines. But I./JG 1's successes were more than double that figure. Four of their 16(!) claims – all LeO 451 bombers bar one – had been made by Hauptmann Wilhelm Balthasar. This took his overall total to 21, one more than the 20 which had won Hauptmann Werner Mölders of III./JG 53 the *Jagdwaffe's* first Knight's Cross a week earlier.

By 9 June, with the French retreat gaining momentum, the *Geschwader's* scene of operations had moved southwards to the lines of the Rivers Aisne and Marne. It was on this date that Adolf Galland scored the last two of the dozen victories he would claim while flying with the *Stabsschwarm* of JG 27, for he had already received notice of his appointment as *Gruppenkommandeur* of III./JG 26.

That same 9 June saw five more French machines added to I./JG 27's collective list of kills. It also witnessed II./JG 27's last major engagement with *Armée de l'Air* fighters. Although the German pilots downed four of the enemy Moranes, they lost six of their own *Emils*. The two pilots killed, Unteroffiziere Hans Siegemund and Lothar Hettmer, shared the unhappy distinction of being the *Gruppe's* first combat fatalities of the war.

It was almost the final throw of the dice for the French. Opposition in the air was fading fast. Another dozen French machines, mainly singletons, were still to be claimed. For the most part, however, Ibel's pilots would spend the closing two weeks of the campaign flying either routine patrols or ground-support sorties.

Sister ship to 'Black 3', 'Black 2' of 5./JG 27 forced-landed east of Lille on 19 May after clashing with RAF Hurricanes. Although behind Allied lines, pilot Leutnant Helmut Strobl managed to evade capture. The very next day he returned to the crash site, now in German hands, where he was photographed with members of an army motorcycle patrol

With 23 aerial victories, plus a further 13 Allied aircraft destroyed on the ground, Hauptmann Wilhelm Balthasar, the *Staffelkapitän* of 1./JG 1, was the most successful Luftwaffe fighter pilot of the French campaign. He was also the first member of JG 27 to be awarded the Knight's Cross

But even a Balthasar could be brought low by engine failure, which appears to be the most likely cause for this otherwise unrecorded belly-landing in a French cornfield. Exact date and location are unknown, but the kill bars just visible on the tail suggest this incident occurred sometime during the second week of June

But there was to be one last flurry of activity from the remnants of the RAF striking force still active in France. On 13 June I./JG 27 shot down six Battles close to the Seine to the south-east of Paris, with II. *Gruppe* adding a seventh. That date also saw I./JG 1 claim a pair of UK-based Blenheims over the same region, plus two French machines.

One of the latter (a Potez 63), together with one of the British bombers, took Hauptmann Wilhelm Balthasar's score to 23. This earned him the Knight's Cross. The *Staffelkapitän* of 1./JG 1 thus became only the second fighter pilot to receive this prestigious award. In fact, Balthasar's performance was to make him the most successful pilot of the campaign, for, in addition to his 23 aerial victories, he also destroyed 13 enemy aircraft on the ground.

A number of Balthasar's ground victories may well have been claimed on 17 June, when I./JG 1 carried out a strafing attack on Chateauroux airfield which resulted in the destruction of 35 French machines. Hoping to repeat this success, the *Gruppe* returned to the same field the following day, only to lose Unteroffiziere Hans Brandt and Fritz Stahn, whose Bf 109s collided during a low-level pass.

Whatever minor damage may have been suffered, Hauptmann Balthasar's 'White 1' was quickly repaired. For this is the same machine (despite the nose numeral being all but obscured by the reflected glare of the strong sunlight on the cowling) being garlanded by its groundcrew, presumably to celebrate the announcement of the Knight's Cross on 14 June. So attached was Balthasar to this particular *Emil* (Wk-Nr. 1559) that he even took it with him when he was appointed *Gruppen kommandeur* of III./JG 3 at the end of August 1940 (see *Osprey Aircraft of the Aces 11 - Bf 109D/E Aces 1939-41*)

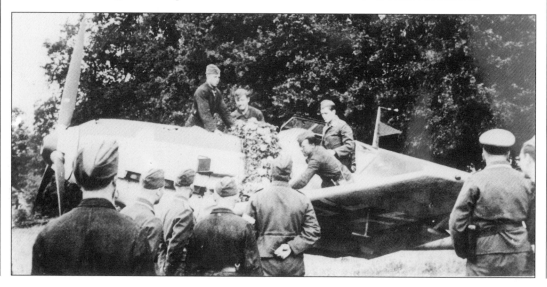

Previously thought to have been of the Battle of Britain period, it is now believed that Leutnant Julius Neumann of 6./JG 27 took this photograph of his fellow *Schwarm* members somewhere high over central France as II. *Gruppe* covered the German advance down to the Loire. Another pilot with a more illustrious namesake (Eduard Neumann, a future *Kommodore* of JG 27), Julius Neumann was to crash-land on the Isle of Wight some two months after this picture was taken. By contrast, his wingman Unteroffizier Fritz Gromotka, here flying 'Yellow 10', would be wearing the Knight's Cross and commanding 9. *Staffel* by war's end

These were the last casualties suffered by Ibel's *Gruppen* during the *Blitzkrieg* in the west – just as the Curtiss Hawk 75 shot down that same day by I./JG 27 was the last victory.

Twenty-four hours later Ibel's force was split in two. While his *Geschwaderstab* and I./JG 1 were ordered to patrol the airspace south of the Seine, I. and II./JG 27 followed the German armies in their pursuit of the French down towards the River Loire.

Neither side saw any action of note during this final week of the campaign. France's Marshal Pétain had first announced his appeal for an armistice on 17 June. It was signed at Compiègne five days later. And at 0035 hrs on 25 June the General Cease Fire was sounded.

Although nobody was aware of the fact at the time, the pilots of JG 27 had just participated in the one major, victorious campaign they would experience throughout their entire history.

Given that von Richthofen's Stukas had played such a pivotal role in both the Polish and French campaigns, it is perhaps not surprising that they were tasked with spearheading the assault on the next enemy – Great

Another neatly executed belly-landing where not only date and location, but also the name of the perpetrator is not known with any certainty. The only clue is the length of that horizontal bar behind the fuselage cross. This was typical of the markings carried by the machines of JG 27's *Geschwaderstab*. This may therefore depict the somewhat undignified end of an internal flight by Oberstleutnant Max Ibel himself sometime during the Battle of Britain (note the mottled camouflage and yellow cowling)

Britain. Even before the last shots in France had been fired, VIII. *Fliegerkorps* was stood down. The operations planned for 20 June were cancelled, and the *Korps* was ordered instead to make ready for transfer northwards to the Normandy coast.

The bulk of JG 27 followed the Stukas up to the Channel a few days later. But soon Oberstleutnant Ibel's Bf 109s would no longer be operating under von Richthofen's direct control. Each of the two air fleets scheduled to take the fight to the enemy's shores – *Luftflotte* 2 over the eastern half of the English Channel and *Luftflotte* 3 to the west – deployed all their single-engined fighters in separate commands. JG 27 would thus join JGs 2 and 53 to form part of *Fliegerführer* 3, the fighter component of *Luftflotte* 3, which was to be headquartered alongside VIII. *Fliegerkorps* at Deauville.

There was little sense of urgency about the gathering of Luftwaffe forces along the shores of the Channel. *Stab* JG 27 and I./JG 1, fresh from patrolling the Seine, flew in to Plumetot, north of Caen, on 30 June. But I. and II./JG 27, whose support of the ground troops in the closing stages of the campaign in France had taken them to the upper reaches of the Loire, had been rotated back to Germany on 28 June.

I. *Gruppe's* stay at Bremen was brief in the extreme. By 3 July it had joined Ibel's *Stab* at Plumetot (I./JG 1 having been transferred to Carque-but on the Cherbourg peninsula 24 hours earlier). In contrast, II./JG 27, after a fortnight's rest and recuperation in the homeland, would spend the next month on coastal defence duties in Holland.

The *Geschwader's* pilots were as about to embark on a very different kind of war. They would be facing a determined, well-organised and well-directed enemy able to display a singleness of purpose which had been denied to the Allied forces in France, whose own operations had been dictated to a great extent – and usually adversely – by the events unfolding on the ground below them.

There was another major difference. The water now in front of them was neither canal nor river, but a 100-mile (160 km) stretch of open sea. To say the Luftwaffe's fighters were unprepared for this hurdle is no understatement. Leutnant Werner Stahl was a member of JG 27's signals section;

'Cross-Channel sorties, involving bitter dogfights over England and a return flight over a large expanse of water, were a great worry to leadership and pilots alike. The difficulties imposed by these operations weighed heavily on all. Our air-sea rescue (ASR) service was still in its infancy. It consisted of a few He 59 floatplanes based in the port of Cherbourg.

'Trials with marker dyes, life-jackets, rescue dinghies and signals equipment were conducted on a daily basis. At first we tried to pinpoint the position of the aircraft in trouble with the most primitive of D/F sets. Later, the new radar installations were to prove of enormous help. The *Kommodore* held daily discussions with his officers, trying to find solutions which would make the *Geschwader* better suited to overwater operations.'

But the schism between the pilots, who had to contend with the problems, and the leadership, who made the demands, remained as wide as ever. As *Kommodore* Ibel was more than once heard to remark in his thick Bavarian accent, 'They may be right, but I for one don't like it!'

One event which Max Ibel presumably *did* welcome took place on 5 July when I./JG 1, which had been an integral part of his *Geschwader* (in all but name) since October 1939, was redesignated and formally placed under his command as III./JG 27. At long last *Jagdgeschwader* 27 had attained full three-*Gruppe* establishment – even if, for the next month, its strength remained divided between Normandy and the Netherlands.

It was time to bite the bullet. And after a few uneventful Stuka-escort missions over the western Channel during the first week of July, the imagined terrors of long overwater flights in single-engined aircraft began to recede. Confidence was further bolstered on the morning of 11 July when Oberleutnant Ludwig Franzisket of 7./JG 27 downed a Hurricane south of Portland. The No 501 Sqn machine was 'Ziskus' Franzisket's tenth kill of the war – and the *Geschwader's* first confirmed victory in the Battle of Britain.

On 5 July 1940 the East Prussian I./JG 1 was redesignated to become III./JG 27. Closely formating on his leader's port wing, the pilot of 'Black 3' shows that both the original *Gruppe* badge, and the unit's unique practice of displaying their individual aircraft numbers on the engine cowling, survived the change intact

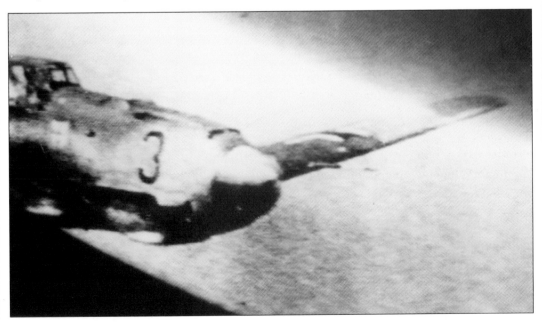

Other successes followed. On 17 July 9./JG 27's Oberleutnant Hans-Folkert Rosenboom, whose account of shooting down a reconnaissance Blenheim in the opening weeks of the war had appeared in the Westphalian newspapers, claimed a similar machine north of Cherbourg. And 48 hours later, while escorting Stukas west of the Isle of Wight, Oberleutnant Walter Adolph's 8./JG 27 reportedly brought down no fewer than five Hurricanes.

But the *Geschwader's* good fortune could not last. On 20 July a pilot of I. *Gruppe* was shot into the sea by Spitfires, and another was forced to ditch. A search was immediately mounted for the missing men. *Gruppenkommandeur* Hauptmann Helmut Riegel took part in the operation, only to be bounced by Hurricanes himself north-west of the island of Alderney. No trace of Helmut Riegel, or of Leutnant Ulrich Scherer, was ever found. Oberfeldwebel Heinz Beushausen's body was later washed ashore in France. As feared, the Channel had claimed its first victims.

Helmut Riegel was the first of five *Gruppenkommandeure* of the luckless I./JG 27 to lose their lives in combat during the course of the war (such were the vagaries of fate that the other *Gruppen* suffered no such fatalities). His successor was ex-*Geschwader*-Adjutant Hauptmann Eduard Neumann who, by chance, had scored his first kill (and the *Stabsschwarm's* only victory of the Battle) – a 236 Sqn Blenheim off Cherbourg – on the very day Riegel was shot down.

Born in a village in the then Austro-Hungarian Duchy of Bukovina, a territory divided between Poland and Rumania after World War 1, the irrepressible 'Edu' Neumann would become one of the leading figures in the history of JG 27, ultimately rising to the position of *Geschwaderkommodore*.

Further skirmishes took place to the south and west of the Isle of Wight during the remainder of July. They resulted in some six claims, but only at the expense of two more pilots being lost over the Channel. One was involved in a mid-air collision with a No 43 Sqn Hurricane some ten miles (16 km) south of the Needles, the other going down off Portland.

By this time *Stab*, I. and III./JG 27 had all moved up to landing grounds in and around Cherbourg, on the northernmost tip of the Cotentin peninsula, thereby shortening their overwater approach route to Portland

When II./JG 27 flew in to Crépon, in Normandy, early in August, its machines were sporting the *Gruppe's* new 'Berlin bear' badge. Note the camouflage netting initially just draped across the wings to hide the conspicuous uppersurface crosses . . .

. . . but which was soon stretched over a framework of poles to provide more complete cover. 'Yellow 3' was the regular mount of Oberleutnant Julius Neumann, who had been the leading light behind Berlin's adoption of II. *Gruppe*. On a visit to the capital's zoo in May 1940 he had even been presented with a live bear, which reportedly later accompanied 6. *Staffel* to the desert

to 'only' some 70 miles (112 km). This was still a long distance to nurse a crippled machine, but it could be done. Unfortunately, it took a twin-engined Coastal Command fighter to prove it, for of the three No 236 Sqn Blenheims claimed by 8./JG 27 near Cherbourg on 1 August (part of a force attacking Querqueville airfield), only two were in fact destroyed. The third limped back to its Thorney Island base damaged, but repairable.

On 5 August II./JG 27 flew in to Crépon in Normandy. During the unit's time spent in defence of the Dutch coastal provinces its pilots had been credited with two Blenheims, but had lost Hauptmann Albrecht von Ankum-Frank, *Kapitän* of 5. *Staffel*, who was shot down during yet another Blenheim raid on II./JG 27's Leeuwarden base just 72 hours before the *Gruppe's* departure for France.

All three of Oberst Ibel's *Gruppen* were engaged in heavy fighting on 8 August. This was centred around a 20-ship coastal convoy which had sailed from the Medway on the previous evening's tide, passed through the Straits of Dover under cover of darkness, and was now heading westwards down the Channel, protected by relays of patrolling RAF fighters.

Von Richthofen's orders to destroy this convoy resulted in three separate Stuka attacks during the course of the day, each escorted by the

The same 'Yellow 3' bellied in on French farmland after a cross-Channel operation sometime in mid-August. It was perhaps damage suffered in this incident which led to 'Jupp' Neumann's flying 'Yellow 6', the machine he was forced to put down on the Isle of Wight on 18 August after a spot of bother with a No 43 Sqn Hurricane

Bf 109s of JG 27. In all, the *Geschwader* would mount 31 missions, involving 261 individual sorties! The *Gruppen* enjoyed mixed fortunes:

'Edu' Neumann's I./JG 27 claimed one Spitfire and one Hurricane on each of the mid-morning and early afternoon raids. During the latter, however, three of its own fighters were shot down south of the Isle of Wight, two pilots being killed.

II./JG 27 did not score until the later afternoon attack, by which time the survivors of the convoy, scattered by the earlier onslaught, had reassembled and were heading towards Weymouth Bay. But the *Gruppe* paid a heavy price for its single Hurricane. Alerted by radar, the defending RAF fighters intercepted the attack force well to the south of the convoy. Four Bf 109s went down in mid-Channel – one pilot missing – while a fifth was written off in a crash-landing back in France.

With four pilots killed or missing, 8 August would be the *Geschwader's* costliest day of the entire Battle of Britain in terms of combat fatalities. But there was another side to the coin. Four other pilots, who had parachuted into the Channel, and whose names in earlier weeks might well have been added to the list of the dead, had instead been saved by the Luftwaffe's increasingly efficient ASR service. Among them was the *Kommandeur* of II. *Gruppe*, Hauptmann Werner Andres.

Only four ships of convoy CW 9 managed to put into Swanage harbour virtually unscathed. Together with other evidence, such as the Royal Navy's withdrawal of its destroyers from Dover, this convinced the Luftwaffe hierarchy that its first objective of the Battle – the denial of the Channel to British shipping – had been attained. Now final preparations were put in hand for the next stage, which was a prerequisite to the cross-Channel invasion itself – the destruction of the RAF's fighter defences. This was to be achieved by a concerted attack on Fighter Command airfields in southern England, scheduled for 13 August, and code-named *'Adlertag'* ('Eagle Day').

In the four days leading up to the great assault JG 27 continued its now routine bomber escort and patrol duties. These cost the *Geschwader* two pilots missing (lost while covering the withdrawal of bombers from a raid on Portland on 11 August), but resulted in eight victory claims, including one for a Curtiss Hawk – submitted after the above action by a pilot whose previous kill had been a French fighter two months earlier. This had presumably left a lasting impression!

The fiasco of *'Adlertag'*, beset by bad weather and a catastrophic breakdown in communications, is well documented. JG 27's main part in the day's confused activities consisted of escorting a force of 50+ Stukas towards one of the designated-target fighter airfields, which they failed to locate, and returning to France with neither claim nor loss.

It was an entirely different story five days later when Oberst Ibel's Bf 109s were again detailed to escort von Richthofen's Stukas across the Channel. The raid of 18 August was a three-pronged attack directed against Poling radar station and the airfields at Ford and Thorney Island.

Savaged by defending Hurricanes and Spitfires, the Stukas suffered grievously (see *Osprey Combat Aircraft 1 - Ju 87 Stukageschwader 1937-41*). Losses among the dive-bombers would have been even higher had it not been for JG 27's fighters. These offered what protection they could, III. *Gruppe* being credited with the destruction of three RAF fighters over the Sussex coast near Ford, and II. *Gruppe* claiming no fewer than 14 (at least half of which remained unconfirmed) in the fierce clashes which took place between Selsey Bill and the Isle of Wight.

The escort's intervention cost them six of their number. Of the five shot down over the Channel, two were saved. One pilot was fortunate enough to be returned to France by the German ASR services. The other, Leutnant Gerhard Mitsdörffer of 1. *Staffel*, was picked up just off Ventnor by the British. He joined 6./JG 27's Oberleutnant Julius Neumann (no relation to Major 'Edu' Neumann), who had put his burning 'Yellow 6' down in a field near Shanklin, on the Isle of Wight, to become the *Geschwader's* first PoWs of the Battle.

After their disastrous performance on what has since become known as the 'Hardest Day', the Ju 87s were withdrawn from operations. VIII. *Fliegerkorps* was transferred *en bloc* to the Pas de Calais, ostensibly to make good their losses in readiness to resume their tactical support role in the coming cross-Channel invasion, but in reality to sit out the rest of the Battle of Britain in near inactivity.

Its Stuka-escort services no longer required (for the time being, at least), JG 27 was also moved up into the Pas de Calais to add its numbers to the eastern Channel fighter force, *Jagdfliegerführer* 2. Before the *Geschwader* departed Cherbourg, however, *Kommodore* Oberst Max Ibel became the second member of JG 27 to receive the Knight's Cross, awarded on 22 August for his 'outstanding qualities of leadership'.

Three days later the *Geschwader's* first Knight's Cross recipient, Hauptmann Wilhelm Balthasar, who had not added to his score since his string of successes in France, was appointed *Gruppenkommandeur* of III./JG 3. His place as the head of 7./JG 27 was taken by Oberleutnant Erhard Braune, previously of the *Gruppenstab*.

After suffering one final loss off the Isle of Wight on 26 August, JG 27 moved up to the Pas de Calais 48 hours later. Oberst Ibel's *Stab* and III. *Gruppe* took up immediate residence at Guines, one of the complex of fields it had used during earlier operations against Dunkirk. I./JG 27 joined the units there on 31 August, having spent the intervening three days at nearby Peuplingues. Meanwhile II. *Gruppe* had flown in to Fiennes, also close by Guines, to complete the redeployment.

After leaving Normandy II./JG 27 took up residence at Fiennes in the Pas de Calais. Of interest here is the wreckage of at least two Fiat CR.42 fighters which can be seen to the left of the picture – refugees of Belgium's *Aéronautique Militaire* escaped after the fighting of May 1940 and since destroyed? Or two of the vanguard of the fifty *Regia Aeronautica* CR.42s sent by Mussolini to operate alongside the Luftwaffe (as 18./JG 56) on the Channel front that had somehow come to grief before reaching their final destination at Maldegem?

The *Geschwader's* move to the Pas de Calais towards the end of August meant that more and more of its aircraft began to be brought down over south-east England. This – admittedly rather poor – photograph shows one of the first. It is Feldwebel Ernst Arnold's 'Yellow 12' of 3./JG 27, seen under armed guard after bellying in at Faversham on 30 August. The bullet holes in the rear fuselage – presumably the cause of its demise – are clearly visible . . .

... but what cannot be seen in the photograph above is the unusual marking aft of the cockpit. Being closely examined by a soldier and a young boy (the latter, incidentally, typical of the hordes of schoolboys who would descend upon almost every crash-site, however remote, and who usually posed the greatest headache for the armed guards!), this 'scissors + r' device indicates that 'Yellow 12' was not just part of 3. *Staffel*, but was one of the four aircraft of the one-time '*Schwarm* Scherer' (*Schere* being the German word for scissors). Leutnant Ulrich Scherer, the eponymous *Schwarmführer*, had disappeared over the western Channel on 20 July – one of the two pilots for whom *Kommandeur* Helmut Riegel was searching when he himself was shot down

The day of the transfer witnessed what was undoubtedly the oddest of all the *Geschwader's* losses of the Battle. Entrusted with a Gotha Go 145A light communications aircraft of Oberst Ibel's HQ flight, a young NCO pilot lost his bearings after taking off from the Channel Islands and put the small biplane down by mistake on the turf of Lewes racecourse in Sussex!

The move from the widest part of the Channel to the narrowest opened up new possibilities for the pilots of JG 27. They would now be able to penetrate much further inland, or remain for much longer periods, after crossing the enemy's coast. But if severely damaged, it also meant exchanging the gamble of a parachute descent into the sea for the certainty of captivity. Still confident of victory, however, this latter prospect was not regarded as too serious. Many pilots had been shot down and made PoW in France, but nearly all had been released within a matter of weeks. One of the earliest missions over the *Geschwader's* new area of operations – escorting bombers of *Luftflotte* 2 over Kent on 30 August – gave a good indication of what was to come. In exchange for the addition of three Spitfires to II./JG 27's scoreboard, the other two *Gruppen* between them reported one pilot missing and two shot down and captured.

This loss ratio – two PoWs to every fatality – would remain remarkably constant throughout the final weeks of the Battle. In contrast to just the two pilots taken into captivity while serving under *Luftflotte* 3 in the

west, no fewer than 22 would be captured during operations over south-eastern England.

September got off to a promising start. Without loss to themselves, the pilots of II./JG 27 were credited with a further seven Spitfires downed over Kent on the first day of the month, while a 2. *Staffel* pilot – who had shot down three RAF machines during the campaign in France – claimed a rather more dubious Curtiss Hawk (another one!) over London.

But as the month progressed, and the Battle approached its climax, the casualty lists began to lengthen (although claims would continue to outnumber losses by some two to one). On the morning of 6 September, while escorting a heavy raid by *Luftflotte* 2's bombers on Fighter Command sector stations around London, the *Geschwader* claimed a total of nine Spitfires destroyed. With the benefit of hindsight – and post-war records – this has proven to be a classic example of the 'Spitfire snobbery' then prevalent among Luftwaffe aircrew, for of the 13 RAF fighters believed shot down by Bf 109s during this attack, only two were in fact Spitfires, the rest being 'less glamorous' Hurricanes!

Whoever their victims, Ibel's pilots were to pay for their successes. By the end of the day's fighting they had lost four of their own number brought down and taken prisoner, plus two others returned wounded. Among those captured was Hauptmann Joachim Schlichting, *Gruppenkommandeur* of III./JG 27, who, also severely wounded, was forced to abandon his blazing fighter near Tilbury. His successor was the long-serving *Kapitän* of 9. *Staffel*, first appointed back in 1938, Hauptmann Max Dobislav.

On 7 September the Luftwaffe suddenly switched its attacks to London. This totally unexpected move offered a welcome respite to the RAF's hard-pressed fighter airfields. For JG 27, the days that followed brought a succession of claims and/or losses – one or two of each, at most – as they continued to escort *Luftflotte* 2's bomber formations or flew *freie Jagd* ('free-hunting') fighter sweeps over south-east England.

Even 15 September, which saw the heaviest fighting of all and is now celebrated annually in the UK as 'Battle of Britain Day', was to prove no exception. Escorting the Do 17s of KG 76 in the first of two major raids on London on that date, I. *Gruppe* lost just two pilots. One forced-landed near Uckfield, in Sussex, possibly brought down by a No 19 Sqn Spitfire,

I./JG 27 was based at Guines throughout September. The rural tranquillity of this scene, with one of the Gruppe's *Emils* nestling cosily in its blast-pen of freshly gathered bales of straw, belies the ferocity of the air war then raging on the other side of the Channel. Note the trailer on the right. This is believed to be the French ex-travelling-circus caravan which *Kommandeur* Hauptmann Eduard Neumann 'liberated' for use as combined living quarters and ops room. Boasting a 'salon', bedroom and kitchen, and towed by a captured British artillery tractor, it too – like 6. *Staffel's* bear – would make the journey to the desert

One member of I. *Gruppe* soon to learn just how ferocious the cross-Channel war could be was 'Edu' Neumann's Adjutant, Oberleutnant Günther Bode. This is his 'White Chevron', minus the *Afrika* badge, pictured earlier in the year (Bode had first been appointed *Gruppen*-Adjutant to Hauptmann Helmut Riegel on 1 February) . . .

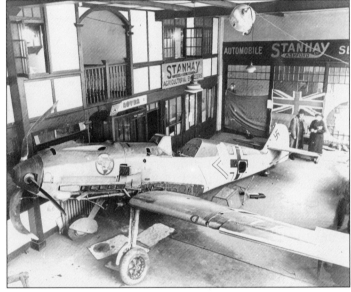

. . . and here it is on display in an Ashford car dealer's showroom, doing its bit for the British war effort despite being somewhat bent and battered after Bode's forced-landing near Mayfield on 9 September

By September the still relatively pristine *hellblau* finish of Bode's machine was the exception rather than the rule. Most of JG 27's aircraft had now been given some form of dapple camouflage to render them less visible against the ground below, as illustrated here by 1. *Staffel's* 'White 7'

A coat of camouflage paint offered little protection against a well-aimed burst of 0.303-in bullets from a Spitfire, however, as Unteroffizier Andreas Walburger discovered on 15 September when a damaged radiator sent him down near Uckfield. One of only two JG 27 machines lost on 'Battle of Britain Day', it was perhaps fitting that Walburger's 'Black 5' should be exhibited in Trafalgar Square. Safely tethered on a Queen Mary trailer, here it sits at the base of (a boarded-up) Nelson's column under the watchful gaze of one of Landseer's four bronze lions . . .

whilst the other disappeared over the Channel. The day's only success was another Spitfire claimed by 6. *Staffel* to the south-east of the capital.

It was not until the end of the month that JG 27 had the next (and last) of its major confrontations of the Battle. On both 27 and 30 September Ibel's *Gruppen* formed part of the massive fighter screens covering bomber formations targeting London. And on both days they took a heavy toll of the defending RAF fighters.

Among I./JG 27's seven victories on 27 September were a brace of Hurricanes – one shot down over Sevenoaks, the other north of Brighton – which were the first two kills for a recently arrived 36-year old Gefreiter (Aircraftsman First Class) of 1. *Staffel*. The oldest operational pilot in the *Geschwader*, Austrian Dr Peter Werfft would end the war a Major and *Kommandeur* of III. *Gruppe*.

. . . but the 2. Staffel *Emil* was made to work for its living. It was also sent on a fund-raising tour of the Home Counties. Here, a local Bedfordshire bobby gets a privileged peek inside the cockpit while the inevitable crowd of schoolboys are kept at bay behind a rope. Later still Werk-Nr 6147 was shipped to America

Framed by a sister machine showing the unmistakable signs of a heavy landing, and somewhat inadequately camouflaged by a single dead branch propped against its spinner, 'Black 11' (and 'red horizontal bar'!) of 5./JG 27 displays an unusual cross-hatch camouflage scheme. This is possibly the aircraft which took Gefreiter Hans-Dieter John on a one-way ride to Lewes in Sussex on 27 September

I./JG 27's successes had been achieved without cost. Not so II. *Gruppe's* quartet of Hurricanes, which were won at the expense of one pilot killed and one captured reportedly unhurt (but who later died in captivity).

On 30 September II. and III. *Gruppen's* total of six claims, four over London and two over Tunbridge Wells respectively, were offset by three of their pilots being taken into British captivity. I. *Gruppe* was less fortunate on this occasion. Its three victories had to be weighed against two pilots killed near Haywards Heath, and another pair injured back at Guines-West.

This marked the end of I./JG 27's activities over south-east England. The next day, 1 October, it was transferred back to Germany. Subordinated to

Three days later, on 30 September, 7. *Staffel's* Oberleutnant Karl Fischer likewise failed to return when his 'White 9' overturned while attempting a forced-landing in Windsor Great Park. Contrary to popular belief of the time, Fischer had not misjudged his height while attacking a pair of defenceless Anson trainers, but had himself been hit in the radiator and fuel tank during a bomber escort mission to London. Seen here being righted, 'White 9' was later exhibited behind a canvas screen outside the walls of Windsor Castle. An admission charge of sixpence to view the wreckage helped to swell the local Spitfire fund

Stab JG 1, the unit was based at Stade, some 17 miles (28 km) to the west of Hamburg, where its pilots spent the next three uneventful weeks (barring one fatal crash) patrolling the German Bight.

On 21 October I./JG 27 staged back to its old western Channel stamping grounds. Reassigned to *Jafü* 3, the *Gruppe* divided its time, the worsening weather conditions permitting, between protecting the north-west coast of France – flying from the airfield at Dinan, just inland from the Gulf of St Malo – and mounting cross-Channel *freie Jagd* and *Jabo* sorties from the landing grounds on the tip of the Cotentin Peninsula.

These latter operations, by now more than risky, resulted in the *Geschwader's* last two losses of the year. One Bf 109 of 3./JG 27 went into the sea off Portsmouth on 17 November after a brush with RAF fighters. Another, of 2. *Staffel*, suffered engine failure and bellied in on Dorset farmland on 30 November. Both pilots survived to become PoWs.

Three days later Hauptmann 'Edu' Neumann's I./JG 27 returned once again to Germany. This time its destination was Döberitz, west of Berlin, where the unit would spend the remaining winter months guarding the Reich's capital.

Meanwhile, there had been some command changes in the Pas de Calais. II./JG 27, which had moved the short distance from Fiennes to St Inglevert on 24 September (it was said that machines dispersed on Fiennes could be seen from the cliffs of Dover!), was given a new *Kommandeur*.

The many hours Hauptmann Werner Andres had spent in the Channel on 8 August, struggling to keep afloat while he awaited rescue, had taxed his resources to the very limit. Recuperation was proving a lengthy process and, in the interim, the *Gruppe* had been led by acting *Kommandeure*. The second of these, Hauptmann Wolfgang Lippert (ex-*Staffelkapitän* of 3./JG 53), was officially appointed *Kommandeur* on 30 September. After making a full recovery, Werner Andres would go on to command III./JG 3 in Russia.

Leading II./JG 27 during the diminishing activity of October, it was Hauptmann Lippert who would achieve the *Gruppe's* – and, indeed, the *Geschwader's* – final victory of the campaign by claiming a Hurricane over Canterbury on the morning of 1 November. The machine, flown by the

Among October's earliest casualties was Unteroffizier Paul Lege of 5./JG 27, seen here leaning against the machine in which he was killed in action against No 605 Sqn Hurricanes near Heathfield. The two victory bars visible on the tailfin would seem to suggest that this photograph was taken on the day he was lost, for the second of his two kills – both Hurricanes – was scored during the second of the three *Jabo* escort sorties flown against London on that 7 October. He was shot down during the third mission by No 605 Sqn's Flt Lt 'Archie' McKellar, who would himself be brought down by Lege's *Gruppenkommandeur*, Hauptmann Wolfgang Lippert, less than a month later – see text

CO of No 605 Sqn, Sqn Ldr 'Archie' McKellar, a leading RAF ace, crashed some five miles (eight kilometres) to the south-east of Kent's cathedral city. Five days later II./JG 27 was withdrawn from France to spend the next two months resting and refitting at Detmold, in Germany.

October also brought a change at the head of the *Geschwader*. Oberst Max Ibel, who had escaped Göring's infamous mid-Battle 'witch-hunt' – dismissing some of his older fighter *Kommodoren* and replacing them with more aggressive 'Young Turks' like Adolf Galland and Hannes Trautloft – now departed to take command of a fighter school (JFS 4) at Nuremberg-Fürth. But he would subsequently return to the Channel front in mid-1941 as *Jafü* 3.

Major Bernhard Woldenga stepped into the breach for 12 days as acting *Kommodore* before Hauptmann Wolfgang Schellmann, hitherto *Geschwaderkommodore* of JG 2, assumed formal command on 22 October. The *Stab* then departed Guines on 10 November to join II. *Gruppe* at Detmold.

Hauptmann Max Dobislav's III./JG 27 took leave of Guines on 10 November too. During their final month in the Pas de Calais the *Gruppe's* pilots had managed to claim five kills. In return, one pilot was reported missing over the Channel and two were captured after coming down in Kent. The latter were the only two *Staffelkapitäne* lost to the *Geschwader* throughout the entire Battle. Both of 8./JG 27, Oberleutnants Günther Deicke and Anton Pointner had taken to their parachutes over the Maidstone area just 12 days apart.

III. *Gruppe's* destination in Germany was Vechta. While there, a small footnote would be added to the story of III./JG 27's service on the Channel front. On 14 December it was announced that the previous *Kommandeur*, Hauptmann Joachim Schlichting, had been awarded the Knight's Cross for his 'exemplary fulfilment of escort duties at the selfless sacrifice of personal victories'. Schlichting, the senior of JG 27's three *Gruppenkommandeure*, had frequently led the whole *Geschwader* on operations until he was shot down at 1800 hrs on 6 September by Flt Lt Norman Ryder of No 41 Sqn off the coast of Shoeburyness, Essex. Schlichting baled out with slight injuries, having become the fifth of Ryder's 7.5 kills – of which were claimed during the course of 1940. The presentation was made to Schlichting, with due ceremony, while in British captivity. A little over a year later, on 31 October 1941, Ryder was himself shot down by flak over France and made a PoW.

Puzzle picture No 1 – the last of the *Geschwader's* losses for 1940 was Unteroffizier Paul Wacker of 2. *Staffel*, forced down by engine failure on Woodyhide Farm alongside the Swanage-Corfe Castle railway line (see embankment in background) on 30 November. But note the very un-JG 27-like markings! 'White G' was obviously an aircraft of II.(Schl.)/LG 2, now a fighter-bomber unit, and one for which the *Geschwader* had often provided fighter cover in the recent past (e.g. Paul Lege's last three missions, detailed on the previous page). So what was Wacker doing flying such a machine? Was he on temporary secondment to II.(Schl)/LG 2, were I./JG 27 so short of bomb-carrying aircraft that they had to borrow one from the *Schlachtgruppe*, or was Wk-Nr. 6313F an ex-*Schlacht* machine newly repaired (as the suffix 'F' indicates) and assigned to I. *Gruppe*, who had not yet had time to repaint it?

MARITA AND BARBAROSSA

The one event of major significance to occur during the winter months – although nobody realised it at the time – was the arrival at Döberitz in January 1941 of a young Oberfähnrich (senior officer cadet). The majority, in fact, regarded it as a non-event, for the newcomer's reputation had preceded him. Although he had claimed seven Spitfires during the Battle of Britain, he had himself been forced to bale out no fewer than six times. He was also seen as something of a maverick, both in the air and on the ground. A 'perpetual violator of flying discipline', his conduct sheet was littered with minor military misdemeanours.

Serving first with I.(J)/LG 2, he was soon transferred to II./JG 52. There, the 21-year-old Berliner – who was, of course, Hans-Joachim Marseille – quickly fell foul of his new *Staffelkapitän*, Oberleutnant Johannes Steinhoff. Six years older, and a career officer who had first joined the *Kriegsmarine* in 1934, Steinhoff found it hard to tolerate Marseille's attitude and unsoldierly bearing. His Bohemian big-city mannerisms, the penchant for wearing his hair longer than most and his 'built-in aversion to military ideals' were all anathema to the *Kapitän* of 4./JG 52;

'Marseille was very handsome. He was a gifted fighter pilot – but he was unreliable. He had girlfriends all over the place, and they kept him so busy that, at times, he was so worn out he had to be grounded. The sometimes irresponsible manner in which he carried out his duties was the main reason I fired him.'

The 'firing' consisted of shunting Marseille off to I./JG 27. *Gruppenkommandeur* 'Edu' Neumann;

Local villagers are attracted by the arrival of III./JG 27's *Emils* in Rumania – possibly Giulesti – early in 1941. The name of the pilot of 'White 2', who has a single victory under his belt (note the kill bar to the left of the swastika), is unfortunately not known

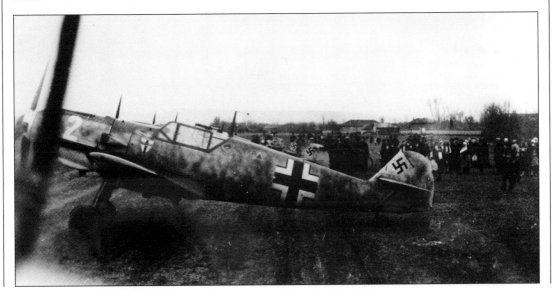

'When Marseille came to JG 27 he brought with him a very bad military reputation, and he was not at all a very likable character. He tried to show off, and considered his knowing a lot of glamorous film stars to be of great importance.'

But in Africa Marseille's character and outlook were to change completely. Far from the fleshpots, his previous misbehaviour came to be regarded more as eccentricity, which did much to enliven the boredom of the desert for his fellow pilots. And the original seven victories would be parlayed into a final total of 158 – the highest number ever scored against the Western allies alone. It is interesting to speculate just what the sharpshooting Marseille's ultimate number of kills might have been had 'Mäcki' Steinhoff been a little more tolerant, and the future 'Star of Africa' had accompanied II./JG 52 to the eastern front instead!

But fame and glory lay some months ahead. When I./JG 27 transferred from Döberitz down to Munich towards the end of February 1941, Ober-fähnrich Hans-Joachim Marseille was simply a junior member of Ober-leutnant Gerhard Homuth's 3. *Staffel* – and still very much on probation.

Stab, II. and III. *Gruppen* had all vacated their winter quarters in Germany some four weeks previously. Early February found them gathered at Baneasa, the combined military and civil airport on the outskirts of the Rumanian capital, Bucharest. This country had already attached itself firmly to the Axis camp, and when neighbouring Bulgaria followed suit on 1 March, Major Schellmann quickly led his two *Gruppen* down into the territory of Germany's newest ally.

But Hitler's hopes of creating a united Axis *bloc* in the Balkans (to cover his southern flank during the coming invasion of the USSR) were dashed by

Hauptmann Hans-Joachim Gerlach, *Staffelkapitän* of 6./JG 27, poses with his Bf 109E at Detmold in the winter of 1940/41. After claiming a pair of RAF Blenheims, Gerlach would become II. *Gruppe's* only casualty of the Balkan campaign, parachuting into captivity on 14 April 1941

an anti-government uprising in Yugoslavia. The Führer therefore decided to resolve the region's problems by force of arms, first crushing Yugoslavian resistance and then going to the aid of his Italian ally, Mussolini, whose five-month-old invasion of Greece had long been in difficulties.

From their Bulgarian bases at Belica and Vrba the Bf 109s of JG 27 were ideally positioned to cover the German air and ground forces already assembling for the attack on Greece, and now tasked with the conquest of Yugoslavia as well. It was as if the Battle of Britain had never been. Operation *Marita*, launched on the morning of 6 April 1941, was pure *Blitzkrieg*.

Once again, the *Geschwader's* twin roles were to secure enemy airspace, thereby allowing their old comrades-in-arms, the Stukas of VIII. *Fliegerkorps*, to operate unmolested. The unit was also to provide close support for the armoured divisions of 12. *Armee* as they advanced out of the mountain passes along the Bulgarian border westwards into Yugoslavia and southwards into Greece.

But there would be *some* parallels to the Battle of Britain. As in the earlier campaign, the *Geschwaderstab* was credited with just one victory. This time it was the *Kommodore* himself who claimed a Hurricane (of No 80 Sqn RAF) near Tanagra, in southern Greece, a fortnight into the fighting. Schellmann's pilots were now also flying an increasing number of *Jabo* (fighter-bomber) missions – a development which had first been imposed upon them during the latter stages of their cross-Channel operations.

Hauptmann Lippert's II. *Gruppe* achieved all 19 of its successes during the second week of *Marita*, by which time the British and Commonwealth forces, which had been rushed to the assistance of the Greeks, were already beginning their fighting withdrawal southwards to the evacuation beaches of Piraeus and the Peleponnese.

Unteroffizier Friedrich Grimpe (foreground) watches as 7. *Staffel* groundcrew bomb-up 'White 7' at Belica, in Bulgaria, during the opening stages of Operation *Marita*. Grimpe would be reported missing over Russia in 'White 9' on 28 July 1941

The machines of II. *Gruppe's* two leading scorers are pictured here at Vrba at the start of the campaign in the Balkans. In the centre is the 'Black Double Chevron' of *Gruppenkommandeur* Hauptmann Wolfgang Lippert, whose tally was standing at 16 at the time. The 15 victory bars on the rudder of the aircraft in the foreground identify it as that of Oberleutnant Gustav Rödel, *Staffelkapitän* of 4./JG 27. On the original print of this photograph it is just possible to make out that the insignia on the first of the bars is Polish. Rödel's first claim, made as a member of 2./JG 21, was for a PZL 'P.24' (in fact, almost certainly a P.11) downed over Warsaw on 1 September 1939

On 13 April, while on a transfer flight from Vrba down to Bitolj, on the Yugoslav-Greek border, 6./JG 27 chanced upon a formation of six unescorted RAF Blenheim bombers and downed every one of them in the space of just four minutes. *Staffelkapitän* Hauptmann Hans-Joachim Gerlach and two of his NCO pilots each claimed a brace of the No 211 Sqn machines.

The following day netted a single Gladiator, but saw the loss of Hans-Joachim Gerlach, who parachuted into captivity when his Bf 109 was hit by ground fire during a strafing attack. Twenty-four hours later still it was the turn of 2./JG 27, which accounted for six Greek fighters during a 15-minute melée near Trikkala. *Staffelkapitän* Oberleutnant Gustav Rödel got two PZL P.24s and a Bloch 151 (which he identified at the time as a Hurricane). Another PZL and a pair of Gladiators completed the haul.

The *Gruppe's* final victories of the campaign were all Hurricanes. The last four of all (three going to Gustav Rödel to bring his total to twenty) were claimed on 20 April, the day II./JG 27 moved down to Larissa, a Greek field only recently evacuated by the RAF.

III./JG 27's fortunes during *Marita* were quite different. Not only did it fail to achieve a single kill, it also suffered the *Geschwader's* only two combat fatalities. 8. *Staffel* was engaged in a *Jabo* attack on Greek positions in the Rupel Pass on the opening morning of the offensive when it was bounced by Hurricanes of No 33 Sqn RAF. Four of the eight Bf 109s went down. One of the two pilots killed was Oberleutnant Arno Becker, the third *Staffelkapitän* of the luckless 8./JG 27 to be lost in a row.

By 26 April *Stab*, II. and III. *Gruppen* were all reunited at Athens-Eleusis, the last stop on their advance through Greece. Here, Schellmann's pilots were able to spend a few relaxing days waiting for the ground columns to catch up with them, before they turned their faces north once more and headed back to Germany, and thence into Poland for the forthcoming assault on the Soviet Union.

But III./JG 27's departure was postponed for a couple of weeks when the *Gruppe's* Bf 109s were ordered to Gela in early May. From this field on Sicily's southern coast, they participated briefly in the Axis air offensive against Malta, some 75 miles (120 km) out into the Mediterranean. Flying a variety of bomber-escort, *freie Jagd* and *Jabo* missions, III./JG 27 made up for its lack of success over Greece by downing five Hurricanes above and around the beleaguered island. One, of No 185 Sqn RAF, was claimed by *Gruppenkommandeur* Hauptmann Max Dobislav on 15 May. The other four all fell victim to the *Gruppe's* leading scorer, Oberleutnant Erbo *Graf* von Kageneck, the *Kapitän* of 9. *Staffel*, which took his total to 17 kills.

Hauptmann Neumann's I./JG 27 also saw action over Malta, although in its case deployment to Sicily had taken place *before*, rather than after, the campaign in the Balkans. And it was of even shorter duration, for the *Gruppe's* fighters were based at Comiso for only the first ten days of March, resulting in the destruction of just one RAF Hurricane.

Having returned to Munich by mid-March, I./JG 27 was soon on the move again. On 4 April it transferred to Graz-Thalerhof, in southern Austria. Temporarily subordinated to *Stab* JG 54, this was to be the unit's base for the invasion of Yugoslavia, launched just 48 hours later.

With the snow-capped peaks of the Olympus range forming a backdrop, and the remains of an RAF Blenheim on the left, 'Yellow 2' of 9./JG 27 poses in textbook *Marita* markings of yellow cowling, narrow mid-fuselage band and rudder at Larissa, in Greece, in April 1941

After the conquest of Greece III./JG 27 was transferred to Gela in Sicily in early May to play a brief part in the air offensive against Malta. Here, *Gruppenkommandeur* Max Dobislav is seen walking by deep in thought as 8. *Staffel's* 'Black 5' is readied for the next mission

45

An E-7 of the *Gruppenstab* awaits refuelling at Gela. Note that although the yellow cowling and rudder have been retained, the washable yellow mid-fuselage band of *Marita* has given way to a broader white aft-fuselage band, denoting service in the Mediterranean theatre. In the background, and similarly marked, are a pair of desert-camouflaged E-7/trops of I./JG 27, presumably *en route* for North Africa

Like the bulk of the *Geschwader* then ranged along Yugoslavia's south-eastern frontiers, I./JG 27 to the north had a dual role to perform in the opening phase of the campaign – neutralisation of the enemy (Yugoslav) air force, and support of its own advancing ground forces. These tasks yielded no aerial victories, but did cost the *Gruppe* the loss of one Bf 109, plus another slightly damaged.

The fighter lost was that flown by 2. *Staffel*'s Leutnant Willi Kothmann, who had claimed the sole Hurricane over Malta a month earlier. Hit by anti-aircraft fire just beyond the Yugoslav border, Kothmann was initially listed as missing, but was soon able to make his way overland back to Graz.

The other casualty was also a victim of ground fire, sustained during 3./JG 27's strafing attack on a clutch of elderly Yugoslav Potez 25 biplanes parked on Ljubljana airfield. The pilot, a certain young Berliner, returned to base without further trouble, however, as recounted by his wingman Unteroffizier Rainer Pöttgen;

Operating already tropicalised *Emils* out of Austria, I./JG 27's role in *Marita* had been confined to the northern regions of Yugoslavia. Two machines were damaged on 6 April 1941. One took a hit from ground fire but returned safely to base, its pilot, an as-yet unknown Oberfähnrich Hans-Joachim Marseille, pointing unconcernedly at the gaping hole above the supercharger air intake

'I was flying 100 metres behind Oberfähnrich Marseille and saw his machine take a flak hit on the left side. But he landed without incident back at Graz with the rest of us.'

After these alarms of the first day, the remainder of I. *Gruppe*'s brief campaign in the Balkans was uneventful. On 11 April it moved down to Agram (Zagreb), the capital of the newly occupied northern part of Yugoslavia, which had declared itself the 'Independent State of Croatia' the day before.

By 14 April the *Gruppe* was back once more in Munich, but again not for long. Less than a week later 'Edu' Neumann's pilots began to retrace their steps down the length of Italy. This time I./JG 27 did not stop at Sicily, but continued on over the Mediterranean to Ain-el-Gazala in North Africa – the setting for undoubtedly the most illustrious chapter in the *Geschwader's* entire history.

Before *Stab*, II. and III. *Gruppen* joined I./JG 27 in the desert, they first had a part to play in Operation *Barbarossa*, the invasion of the USSR. Having returned from Greece (and Sicily) some weeks earlier, by mid-June 1941 Major Schellmann's units found themselves close to the ex-Polish border with Lithuania, awaiting the start of their third *Blitzkrieg*. For the assault on the Soviet Union was to be yet another repeat of the Wehrmacht's tried and tested tactics, albeit on a much more epic scale than any of the earlier campaigns.

Reinforced by the temporary addition of II./JG 52 and III./JG 53 (the former, ironically, Marseille's old unit), JG 27 once again formed the single-engined fighter component of the now General von Richthofen's VIII. *Fliegerkorps*. And, once again, their primary function would first be the elimination of enemy air power. But never before had the Luftwaffe faced an opponent of such numbers. Therefore, in addition to their traditional Stuka-escort duties, many of JG 27's pilots would spend the opening hours of *Barbarossa* flying a series of ground attack sorties against numerous Soviet frontier airfields.

The other aircraft 'damaged' on 6 April was apparently the victim of an accidental fire while on the ground at Graz-Thalerhof. Curiously, the daily loss returns assessed the damage at 40 per cent – an administrative slip of the pen, or an overconfident engineering section?

A new weapon was introduced to assist them in their task. It consisted of large ventral bomb-rack fairings which could be fitted to the belly of their Bf 109s. Each of the fighters so equipped was capable of carrying 96(!) SD-2 *Splitterbomben*. These tiny fragmentation bomblets, weighing only 2 kg (4.4 lbs) apiece, had originally been developed as an anti-personnel weapon. But they were to prove highly effective when used against rows of parked Soviet aircraft. Unfortunately, they also posed no little risk to the pilots dropping them (see *Osprey Aircraft of the Aces 37 - Bf 109 Aces of the Russian Front*).

Launched in the early hours of 22 June 1941, *Barbarossa's* initial air strikes were even more successful than the planners had dared hope. Heavily committed to these early *Jabo* raids on the forward bases of the unsuspecting Red Air Force, II. and III./JG 27's combined total of aerial kills on the first day was perforce a modest (by eastern front standards) 13.

But, for the *Geschwader* as a whole, 22 June would be dominated by the loss of their *Kommodore*. One of the *Stabsschwarm* later described what happened;

'Near Grodno we came under fire from flak. Schellmann shot down a Rata, but some of the pieces flying off it must have hit the *Kommodore's* machine. We saw Schellmann take to his parachute.'

No further trace of Major Wolfgang Schellmann was ever found. It is widely believed that he was captured and shot some 48 hours later by the NKVD. The I-16 Rata mentioned above was his 14th kill of the war, just two of which had been claimed while commanding JG 27.

Portrayed here during the *Marita* operation – the tropical headgear suggesting perhaps the latter stages in southern Greece – Major Wolfgang Schellmann, *Geschwader-kommodore* of JG 27 since October 1940, would be lost on the opening day of *Barbarossa*

Wolfgang Schellmann would be the only *Kommodore* of JG 27 to be lost in action. His immediate replacement was no stranger to the *Geschwader*. Major Bernhard Woldenga was the officer who had activated the original I./JG 131 (now III./JG 27) back in March 1937. Having commanded JG 77 for the past six months, he celebrated his return in fine style by claiming his first ever victory – a twin-engined Tupolev bomber, near Vilna – on 25 June.

The new *Kommodore* would add three more kills to his score during the remainder of *Stab* JG 27's four-month stint on the eastern front. Woldenga would also receive the Knight's Cross (on 5 July) for his leadership of JG 77 during the recent Balkan and Cretan campaigns. But by far the lion's share of the *Stab's* victims (eight out of the overall total of thirteen) on the eastern front fell to the vastly experienced Oberfeldwebel Erwin Sawallisch.

Another Knight's Cross had been awarded on the opening day of *Barbarossa*. The recipient was Oberleutnant Gustav Rödel, *Staffelkapitän* of 4./JG 27, who had claimed his 20th kill towards the close of the campaign in Greece. Rödel would add another while on the eastern front. This latest victim was but one of the 25(!) Soviet bombers which II. *Gruppe* shot out of the sky around Vilna on 25 June. Seven others were credited to 5. *Staffel's* Leutnant Gustav Langanke, whose only previous victory had been a Hurricane brought down over London in September 1940 during the height of the Battle of Britain.

But this tantalising glimpse of the air war in the east, and the high individual scores which could be amassed against the Soviets, was to be all too brief, for shortly afterwards II. *Gruppe* were ordered to hand its aircraft over to III./JG 27. The rigours of the Russian front were already beginning to make themselves felt, for the combined serviceability figures of the two *Gruppen* were scarcely enough to allow one to operate efficiently.

In their nine-day campaign against the Red Air Force, Hauptmann Lippert's II./JG 27 had claimed 42 enemy aircraft destroyed. More than a dozen of their own fighters had been lost or damaged, but the *Gruppe* had suffered only one combat fatality, Oberleutnant Wilhelm Wiesinger having been hit by ground fire during a low-level *Jabo* strike on 23 June.

II. *Gruppe* returned to Döberitz in July. Here, it would spend the next two months re-equipping with new Bf 109Fs, before joining I./JG 27 at Ain-el-Gazala, in Libya, late in September.

During this time III./JG 27 continued to operate alongside the *Geschwaderstab* on the Russian front. As they staged ever further eastwards, moving from one airfield to the next in the wake of Army Group Centre's advance on Moscow, the *Gruppe's* collective scoreboard lengthened dramatically. Measured in numbers of enemy aircraft destroyed, it was probably the most successful period of any in the history of JG 27.

More than two dozen of Hauptmann Dobislav's pilots cut their combat teeth on the road to the Russian capital, gaining the first kills of their careers. Others consolidated previous successes by adding to their growing totals.

But one name above all others runs like a thread throughout III./JG 27's operations on the eastern front. Oberleutnant Erbo *Graf* von Kageneck's 18th kill (a Tupolev bomber south of Vilna) had been claimed on the first day of *Barbarossa*. An Ilyushin DB-3 provided the *Kapitän* of 9. *Staffel*

With 48 Soviet kills, Oberleutnant Erbo *Graf* von Kageneck, *Staffelkapitän* of 9./JG 27, was the *Geschwader's* most successful pilot on the eastern front. This earlier snapshot of the 22-year-old count, then still a Leutnant, bears the inscription 'Erbo before a mission'

with number 37 on 27 July, earning him the Knight's Cross 72 hours later. And a Soviet fighter downed on 12 October – the *Gruppe's* last day in action in Russia – took his total to 65. For this achievement, he became the first member of JG 27 to be awarded the Oak Leaves.

Second only to von Kageneck in the Soviet scoring stakes was an NCO pilot of his own 9. *Staffel*. Oberfeldwebel Franz Blazytko raised his pre-*Barbarossa* quartet of kills to 29 (some sources quote 30) before he was shot down and captured during a *freie Jagd* sweep on 23 September.

Blazytko was the tenth, and last, of the *Gruppe's* pilots to be lost in action on the Russian front. Against this they had claimed no fewer than 224 Soviet aircraft shot down during the four months of fighting which had taken them as far east as Vyazma, only some 120 miles (193 km) from Moscow, as well as northwards towards Leningrad.

In mid-October it was the turn of the *Geschwaderstab* and III./JG 27 to be withdrawn to Döberitz for re-equipment with the Bf 109F. Two months later they too would arrive in Libya, thereby re-uniting the complete *Geschwader* for the first time in more than a year.

Although of indifferent quality, this photograph of von Kageneck's 'Yellow 1' after its forced-landing behind German lines along the Volkhov front to the south-east of Leningrad on 20 August 1941 clearly shows the wide yellow aft-fuselage band of the eastern front. The 45 victory bars on the rudder can also just be made out. The last of these was an 'I-18' (aka MiG-3?) shot down east of Novgorod on 16 August – there obviously had not yet been time to add the next two (also 'I-18s'), claimed 72 hours later

Wearing the red-and-yellow sleeve patch of Spain, these two pilots of 15.(*span.*)/JG 27, clad in gloves and scarves, are all too clearly feeling the approaching chill of the Russian winter. Standing in front of one of their equally well wrapped-up *Emils*, they are displaying the flag of the first *Escuadrilla Azul* (or 'blue squadron', as each of the five successive Spanish volunteer fighter units in Russia was to be known)

But *Stab* and III. *Gruppe*'s departure for Döberitz had not severed JG 27's links with the eastern front altogether. Late in September 1941 a squadron of Spanish volunteers had arrived in Russia after having undergone eight weeks' training at Werneuchen.

Led by *Commandante* (Major) Angel Salas Larrazábal, a Civil War veteran with 16+ victories, this squadron was assigned to Major Woldenga's command, and operated as 15.(*span.*)/JG 27.

Even after *Stab* JG 27's return to Germany, the Spanish unit retained its original designation (although now attached to JG 52). In its five-month combat career on the Moscow front, 15.(*span.*)/JG 27 claimed fourteen enemy aircraft shot down – exactly half being credited to *Commandante* Larrazábal. But it suffered one pilot killed and three missing in action.

In March 1942 the first tour-expired squadron was replaced by a fresh batch of Spanish volunteers. This second *Staffel* was also to have been designated 15.(*span.*)/JG 27, but with Woldenga's *Stab* now long gone, it was instead initially subordinated directly to *Luftflotte* 2. Later it, and three further Spanish volunteer squadrons, would all operate in turn as part of JG 51.

COLOUR PLATES

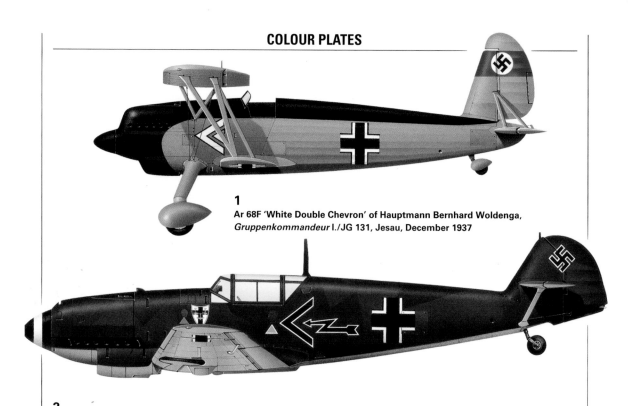

1
Ar 68F 'White Double Chevron' of Hauptmann Bernhard Woldenga,
Gruppenkommandeur I./JG 131, Jesau, December 1937

2
Bf 109D-1 'Black Chevron and Flash' of *Gruppenstab* I./JG 131, Jesau, September 1938

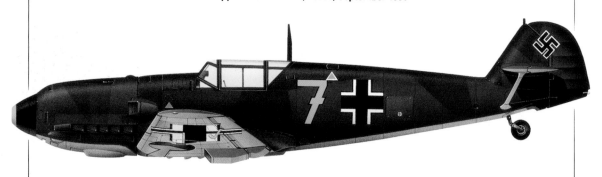

3
Bf 109E-3 'Yellow 7' of 3./JG 27, Münster-Handorf, October 1939

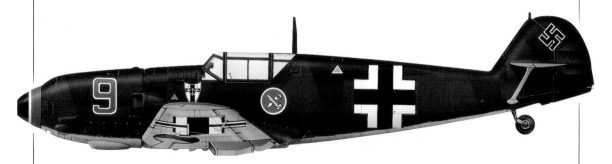

4
Bf 109E-1 'Red 9' of 2./JG 1, Vörden, December 1939

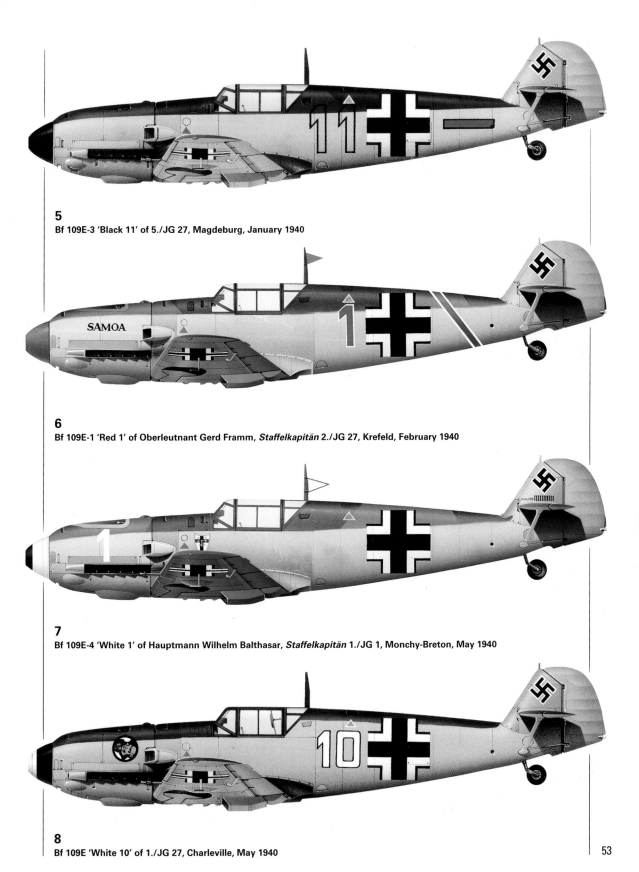

5
Bf 109E-3 'Black 11' of 5./JG 27, Magdeburg, January 1940

6
Bf 109E-1 'Red 1' of Oberleutnant Gerd Framm, *Staffelkapitän* 2./JG 27, Krefeld, February 1940

7
Bf 109E-4 'White 1' of Hauptmann Wilhelm Balthasar, *Staffelkapitän* 1./JG 1, Monchy-Breton, May 1940

8
Bf 109E 'White 10' of 1./JG 27, Charleville, May 1940

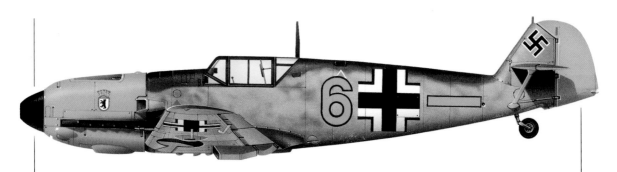

9
Bf 109E 'Yellow 6' of 6./JG 27, Fiennes, September 1940

10
Bf 109E-7 'White 1' of Oberleutnant Wolfgang Redlich, *Staffelkapitän* 1./JG 27, Guines, September 1940

11
Bf 109E-7 'Black 2' of 5./JG 27, Vrba, March 1941

12
Bf 109E-4/B 'Yellow 5' of 6./JG 27, Vilna, June 1941

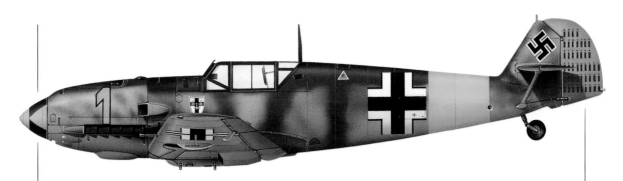

13
Bf 109E-7 'Yellow 1' of Oberleutnant Erbo *Graf* von Kageneck, *Staffelkapitän* 9./JG 27, Solzy, August 1941

14
Bf 109E-7/trop 'Black Chevron A' of Oberleutnant Ludwig Franzisket, *Gruppen*-Adjutant I./JG 27, Ain-el-Gazala,
September 1941

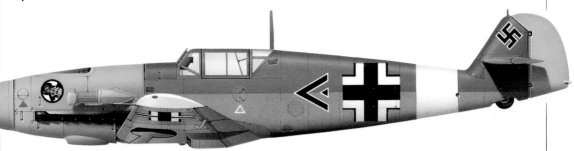

15
Bf 109F-4/trop 'Black Double Chevron' of Hauptmann Eduard Neumann, *Gruppenkommandeur* I./JG 27, Ain-el-Gazala,
November 1941

16
Bf 109F-4/trop 'Black 9' of 5./JG 27, Ain-el-Gazala, December 1941

17
Bf 109F-4/trop 'Black 2' of 8./JG 27, Tmimi, December 1941

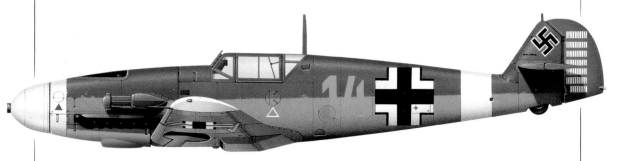

18
Bf 109F-4/trop 'Yellow 14' of Leutnant Hans-Joachim Marseille, 3./JG 27, Tmimi, May 1942

19
Bf 109F-4/trop 'Red 1' of Leutnant Hans-Arnold Stahlschmidt, *Staffelkapitän* 2./JG 27, Quotaifiya, August 1942

20
Bf 109F-4/trop 'Yellow 5' of Leutnant Gerhard Mix, 6./JG 27, Quotaifiya, August 1942

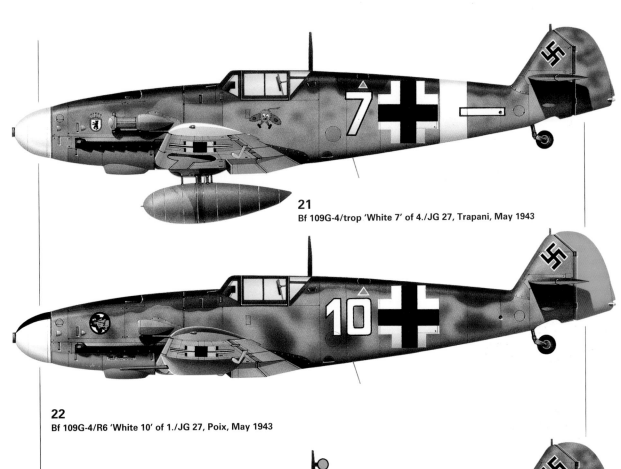

21
Bf 109G-4/trop 'White 7' of 4./JG 27, Trapani, May 1943

22
Bf 109G-4/R6 'White 10' of 1./JG 27, Poix, May 1943

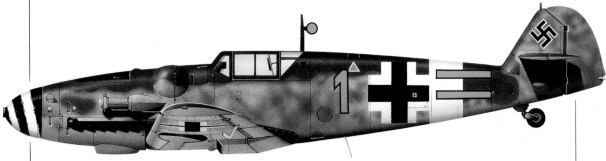

23
Bf 109G-6/trop 'Yellow 1' of Oberleutnant Dietrich Boesler, *Staffelkapitän* 12./JG 27, Tanagra, July 1943

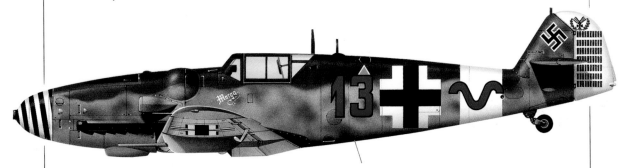

24
Bf 109G-6/R6 'Red 13' of Feldwebel Heinrich Bartels, 11./JG 27, Kalamaki, November 1943

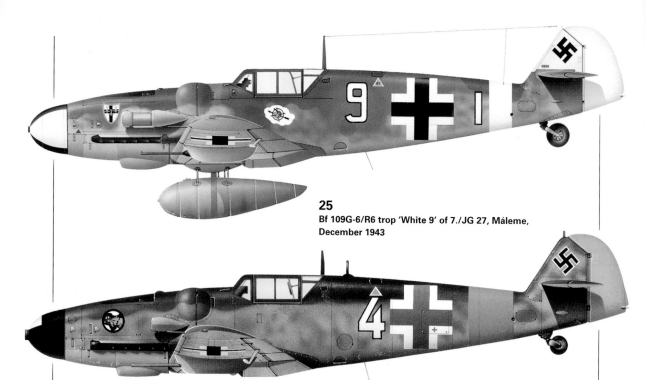

25
Bf 109G-6/R6 trop 'White 9' of 7./JG 27, Máleme,
December 1943

26
Bf 109G-6/R6 'White 4' of 1./JG 27, Fels am Wagram, January 1944

27
Bf 109G-6/R6 'White 23' of 1./JG 27, Fels am Wagram, January 1944

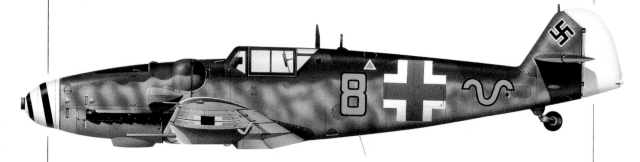

28
Bf 109G-6/R6 'Yellow 8' of 12./JG 27, Skopje, February 1944

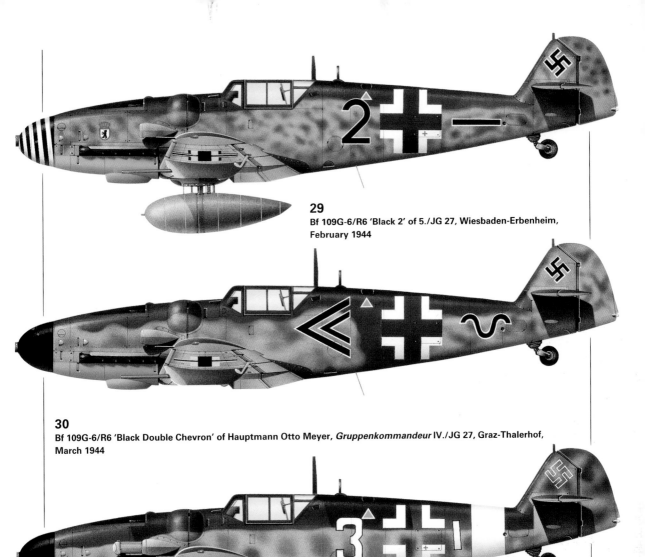

29
Bf 109G-6/R6 'Black 2' of 5./JG 27, Wiesbaden-Erbenheim,
February 1944

30
Bf 109G-6/R6 'Black Double Chevron' of Hauptmann Otto Meyer, *Gruppenkommandeur* IV./JG 27, Graz-Thalerhof,
March 1944

31
Bf 109G-6/R6 trop 'White 3' of Unteroffizier Franz Stadler, 7./JG 27, Máleme, April 1944

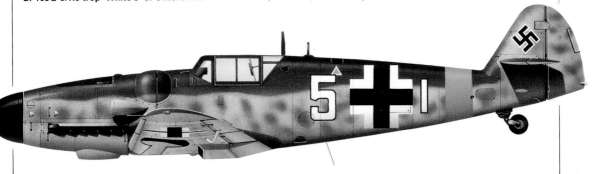

32
Bf 109G-6 'White 5' of 7./JG 27, Connantre, June 1944

33
Bf 109G-6/AS 'Yellow 2' of 6./JG 27, Fels am Wagram, July 1944

34
Bf 109G-14 'White 14' of Oberleutnant Ernst-Georg Altnorthoff, *Staffelkapitän* 13./JG 27, Hustedt, September 1944

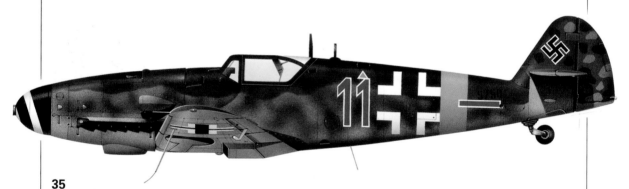

35
Bf 109G-14/AS 'Blue 11' (Wk-Nr. 785750) of 8./JG 27, Rheine-Hopsten, March 1945

36
Bf 109K-4 'Red 18' of 2./JG 27, Bad Aibling, April 1945

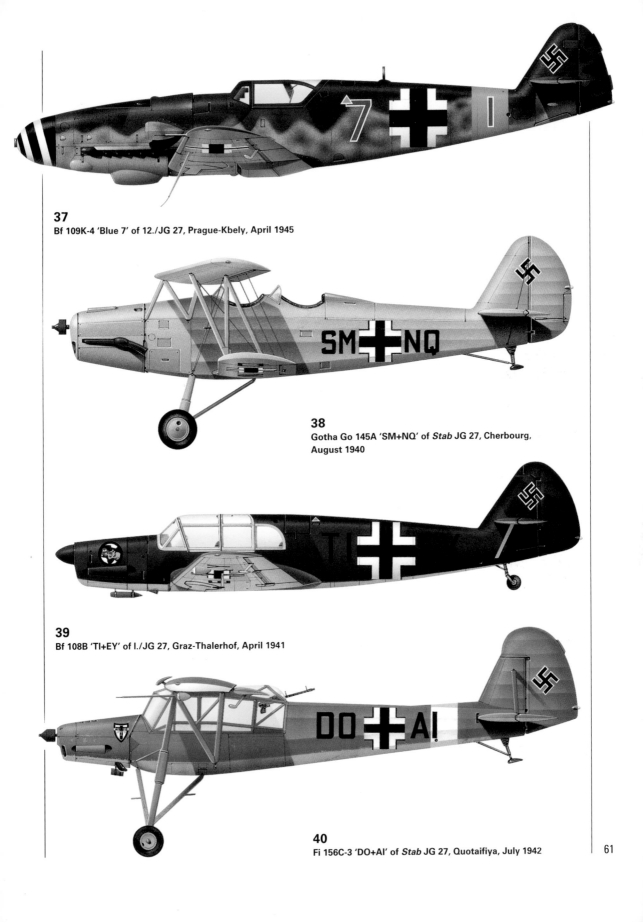

37
Bf 109K-4 'Blue 7' of 12./JG 27, Prague-Kbely, April 1945

38
Gotha Go 145A 'SM+NQ' of *Stab* JG 27, Cherbourg,
August 1940

39
Bf 108B 'TI+EY' of I./JG 27, Graz-Thalerhof, April 1941

40
Fi 156C-3 'DO+AI' of *Stab* JG 27, Quotaifiya, July 1942

1
JG 27
worn on the cowling of the Fi 156
and Bf 109F

2
I./JG 27
worn on the cowling of the Bf 109E,
F and G, Bf 108, Fi 156 and on the
nose of Caudron C.445

3
2./JG 27
worn on the cowling of the Bf 109E

4
3./JG 27
worn on the cowling of the Bf 109G

5
II./JG 27
worn on the cowling of the Bf 109E,
F and G

6
Gruppenstab JG 27
worn below the cockpit of the
Bf 109E/F

7
4./JG 27
worn below the cockpit of the
Bf 109F/G

8
5./JG 27
worn below the cockpit of the
Bf 109F

9
6./JG 27
worn below the cockpit of the
Bf 109G

10
III./JG 27
worn below the windscreen of the
Bf 109D, E and F and on cowling of
the Bf 109F/G

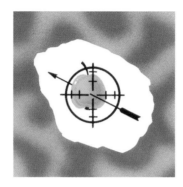

11
7./JG 27
worn below the cockpit of the
Bf 109G

12
8./JG 27
worn below the cockpit of the
Bf 109G

13
9./JG 27?
worn below the cockpit of the
Bf 109G

14
IV./JG 27
worn below the windscreen or on
cowling of the Bf 109G

15
2./JG 1
worn below the cockpit of the
Bf 109E

16
15.(*span.*)/JG 27
worn on the cowling of the Bf 109E-7

17
Erg.Gr.JG 27
worn on the cowling of the Bf 109E

18
Schwarm 'Scherer'
worn behind cockpit of the Bf 109E

AFRICA – THE 'FINEST HOUR'

The presence of the Wehrmacht in North Africa, like its intervention in Greece, was due in no small measure to the military incompetence of Hitler's Axis ally, Mussolini. Just as the Italian invasion of Greece had not merely foundered on the rock of Greek resistance, but had been pushed back into Albania whence it came, so the Italian advance into Egypt in September 1940 was not simply stopped cold by British and Commonwealth troops, it was driven back halfway across Libya to the port of Benghazi and beyond.

It was to prevent the total loss of Italy's African colony that Hitler was persuaded early in 1941 to send a token 'containing' force, built around the 5th Light and 15th Panzer Divisions, to his southern partner's aid. The Führer's plans were purely defensive. He warned the force commander, one Generalleutnant Erwin Rommel, that 'no large-scale operations were to be carried out in North Africa until the autumn'. But Rommel had ideas of his own as to how the desert war should be fought. Realising that the British forces opposing him were both overstretched and understrength, he quickly began to prepare for a 'reconnaissance in force'.

By the time the first elements of I./JG 27 touched down on the cleared stretch of desert that was Ain-el-Gazala airfield on 18 April 1941, Rommel's 'reconnaissance' had exploded into a full-blown offensive. He

Bf 109E-7/trops of 3./JG 27 are seen during a stop-over in Italy while on the transfer flight from Munich down to North Africa in mid-April 1941. Note the long-range ventral fuel tanks, and the white sidewall tyres sported by the machine in the foreground. These latter were reportedly a utilitarian measure intended to protect the rubber from the rays of the sun. But they also befitted the flamboyant nature of the aircraft's pilot – a certain young Berliner just visible in the cockpit at far right

Above
Once arrived in Sicily, preparations were made for the final leg across the Mediterranean to Libya. But something happening off to the left seems to have momentarily distracted this group of 1./JG 27 pilots and interrupted the discussion between *Staffelkapitän* Oberleutnant Wolfgang Redlich (holding maps) and the pilot of the Bf 110 (in peaked cap and flight overalls) who is to lead the formation. At right, wearing the kapok life-jacket, is Feldwebel Albert Espenlaub, who would lose his life while attempting to escape after belly-landing behind Allied lines near El Adem on 13 December 1941

Left
Three more NCO pilots of 1. *Staffel* enjoy a final cigarette each as they await the long overwater haul to Tripoli. Unteroffizier Hans Sippel (left) and Feldwebel Werner Lange (centre) have only days to live. Both would be killed in action against RAF fighters over Tobruk before April was out. Unteroffizier Günther Steinhausen (right) was destined for a posthumous Knight's Cross, awarded for the 40 victories he had achieved before being shot down near El Alamein on 6 September 1942

If one picture is worth a thousand words, then this is perhaps the one – the minaret and the palm trees say it all . . . *Jagdgeschwader* 27 has arrived in North Africa!

JG 27's 'patch' for 20 months is revealed in this map of the North African coastline – the scene of some of the hardest fought battles of World War 2, both on the ground and in the air (*map by John Weal*)

had already retaken all of Libya – with the exception of Tobruk – and his troops had reached the Egyptian frontier at Sollum.

As Hauptmann Eduard Neumann's Bf 109s were the first single-engined Luftwaffe fighters to be sent to Africa, they were thrown into the thick of the fighting almost immediately upon arrival. And with the situation along the Libyan/Egyptian border at a temporary stalemate, this fighting was concentrated around the perimeter of Tobruk, whose garrison – although surrounded – was a thorn in Rommel's side, and a potential threat to his line of supply.

On 19 April I./JG 27 claimed its first four victories – all Hurricanes – along the 37-mile (60-km) stretch of coast separating Gazala from Tobruk. One of the pair shot down by Oberleutnant Karl-Wolfgang Redlich, *Kapitän* of 1. *Staffel*, provided I./JG 27 with its 100th victory of the war. Another was the first kill for Leutnant Werner Schroer, who would end the war as the *Geschwaderkommodore* of JG 3 'Udet', wearing the Swords, and with the distinction of being one of the few Luftwaffe pilots credited with more than 100 RAF and USAAF aircraft destroyed.

The fourth of that day's Hurricanes had gone to Unteroffizier Hans Sippel. Twenty-four hours later he would claim a Wellington, also over

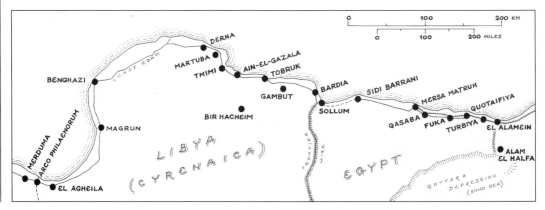

AFRICA – THE 'FINEST HOUR'

The propaganda machine took a more bombastic approach. This official photograph of I./JG 27's *Gruppe* standard being paraded in front of 3. *Staffel's* 'Yellow 4' was intended for home consumption, and aimed to demonstrate the ever-widening sphere of the Luftwaffe's influence . . .

. . . although the reality of everyday life in North Africa was far less formal. The irrepressible Hauptmann Eduard 'Edu' Neumann, *Kommandeur* of I. *Gruppe*, models the preferred outfit of the well-dressed desert airman – tropical helmet and sun goggles (optional), lightweight khaki-brown jacket or shirt, ankle socks and sandals (the latter out of shot)

Gazala, only to become JG 27's first African casualty the day after that when he himself was shot down and killed over Tobruk on 21 April.

It was on 23 April that Oberfähnrich Hans-Joachim Marseille claimed his first success as a member of JG 27 – another Hurricane over Tobruk. This prompted 'Edu' Neumann to remark that 'we'll make a proper fighter pilot out of you yet'. The *Gruppenkommandeur* never spoke a truer word. But with just eight kills under his belt, Marseille was still a long way behind I./JG 27's leading trio of scorers.

These three, Oberleutnants Ludwig Franzisket, Karl-Wolfgang Redlich and Gerhard Homuth, all had totals climbing into the high teens. This meant they were nearing the 'magic 20', which was still the official yardstick for the award of the Knight's Cross – the astronomical scores of the eastern front had yet to make themselves felt! And, indeed, all three would receive the prestigious decoration in the coming weeks.

On the morning of 1 May 3./JG 27 clashed with a squadron of Hurricanes south of Tobruk. *Staffelkapitän* Gerhard Homuth and Hans-Joachim Marseille – the latter now flying as a *Schwarmführer* (leader of a four-aircraft section) – downed a pair of enemy fighters each. By now the few remaining Hurricanes based within the Tobruk perimeter had been withdrawn to Egypt. Their departure coincided with the easing of Rommel's latest, unsuccessful, attempt to overrun the garrison. As both sides paused to draw breath and regroup, the following fortnight saw just three victories for the *Gruppe*, all claimed by Gerhard Homuth.

Freed from the restraints of their Stuka-escort and patrol duties over a now fighterless Tobruk (henceforward the 'fortress' would have to rely almost entirely on its own anti-aircraft defences for protection against air attack), I./JG 27 began to venture further eastwards towards the Egyptian border. And its was here that action flared up again on 21 May when 3. *Staffel* intercepted a raid by Blenheim bombers. They shot down five of the No 14 Sqn machines, two of which took Gerhard Homuth's score to 22 and won him the Knight's Cross.

But such successes against bombers would be very much the exception, rather than the rule, in the months ahead. JG 27's desert war was to remain one of predominantly fighter combat throughout. And four weeks after intercepting the Blenheims – having added a further dozen Hurricanes to its growing scoresheet in the interim – I./JG 27 met for the first time the one Allied fighter which, above all others, was to be its principal opponent, and which alone would account for almost exactly half the 600 kills the *Gruppe* would claim during its time in North Africa.

When 1. *Staffel* bounced a formation of unfamiliar enemy fighters just beyond the Egyptian border in the early morning of 18 June, they logged their three successes simply as 'Brewsters'. In fact, they were Curtiss Tomahawks of the reformed No 250 Sqn RAF. One of the trio was victory number 21 for *Staffelkapitän* Wolfgang Redlich, and resulted in the *Gruppe*'s second African Knight's Cross. It would be another month before the third was awarded. This followed the destruction of a Hurricane (wrongly identified as a Tomahawk!) over the Gulf of Sollum by *Gruppen*-Adjutant Ludwig Franzisket on 19 July.

With two recent British counter-offensives having been repulsed, the stand-off on the ground continued. But now I./JG 27 began to probe even deeper into Egyptian airspace, often staging through Gambut, a complex of airfields closer to the frontier, in order to increase their combat radius.

A later portrait of the then Major Gerhard Homuth who, as an Oberleutnant and *Staffelkapitän* of 3./JG 27, won the *Geschwader's* first desert Knight's Cross with the destruction of two RAF Blenheim bombers south-east of Fort Capuzzo, an Axis stronghold on the Libyan/Egyptian border, on 21 May 1941

The machines of Neumann's two other *Staffelkapitäne* sit parked on Gazala's rock-strewn dispersal area. 'Black 1' in the background is the mount of the recently appointed Hauptmann Erich Gerlitz of 2./JG 27, while the 20 kill bars on the rudder of the *Emil* in the foreground not only reveal it to be that of 1. *Staffel's* Oberleutnant Karl-Wolfgang Redlich ('White 1'), but also pinpoint the date of this photograph as having been taken in mid-June 1941. Redlich's 19th and 20th, both Hurricanes, went down over the Egyptian frontier on 15 June. Number 21, a 'Brewster', was claimed three days later in the same area, and resulted in the Knight's Cross for Redlich

Just over a month later the third Knight's Cross went to *Gruppen-Adjutant* Oberleutnant Ludwig Franzisket. He was serving as acting-*Staffelkapitän* of 3./JG 27 during the temporary absence of Gerhard Homuth when he claimed a Tomahawk (actually a No 73 Sqn Hurricane) on 19 July to take his score to 22. 'Ziskus' Franzisket, who was a Leutnant with I./JG 1 at the start of the war, ended it with 43 victories, and as the sixth and final *Kommodore* of JG 27

The pilots of I./JG 27 may have become accustomed to unprepared grass strips, such as they had encountered during the French and Balkan campaigns, but the sandy expanse of Ain-el-Gazala – dotted with rocks the size of house bricks – was something else entirely. The biggest handicap of all was the clouds of dust sent up by any kind of aircraft movement. Here, 2. *Staffel's* Leutnant Werner Schroer keeps well clear of the sandstorm generated by a previously departing machine as he taxies out in his 'Black 8' for another mission

This aerial shot of a *Schwarm* taking off – each of the four widely spaced machines trailing its own lengthening plume of dust and sand – illustrates the extent of the problem. If this were an emergency scramble, with the field under threat of imminent attack, visibility for those on the ground would be severely curtailed for many vital minutes

Towards the close of a relatively uneventful August the newly promoted Leutnant Hans-Joachim Marseille, who had not scored for over two months, claimed a South African Air Force (SAAF) Hurricane just off the coast of Egypt near Sidi Barrani. It was Marseille's 14th victory. On 9 September he downed two more Hurricanes over Bardia, an important Axis base, and port, 12 miles (19 km) inside the Libyan frontier. On both 13 and 14 September Marseille was credited with single Hurricanes.

And then something extraordinary happened.

Hans-Joachim Marseille himself later described 24 September 1941 as 'the day everything suddenly fell into place'. It was on this date that his innate skills – long suspected by such as Hauptmann Neumann, but never before properly displayed – all fused as one to enable him to shoot down a quartet of Hurricanes and a twin-engined Martin Maryland bomber.

These victories boosted Marseille's score to 23. It would take several more weeks of combat to hone his 'almost uncanny' talents to perfection, but soon the young Berliner's lethal abilities became the stuff of legends: his remarkable eyesight, which meant he could detect the smallest of specks in the far distance vital seconds before anybody else; his complete mastery of aerobatics, which invariably allowed him to place himself in a position of tactical advantage; the ferocity of the assault upon his chosen target; the computer-like instinct which told him the exact moment to open fire in any given situation, however great the angle; the precision marksmanship to hit the vital spot.

In fact, it was later calculated that Marseille required an average of only 15 rounds to despatch an opponent – far fewer than any other Luftwaffe fighter pilot. He often returned from sorties which had netted him multiple

Once aloft, however, it was a different story. According to one pilot who fought there, the western desert was the 'perfect arena for air warfare, with no obstacles, either geographical or man-made, and, more often than not, unlimited visibility'. These *Emils* of 1. *Staffel*, with 'White 3' leading, capture the very spirit of those words as they scythe through the clear air above the featureless wastes

kills – sometimes as many as six – with more than half his ammunition still in its magazines! Many rated him the best shot in the Luftwaffe.

The 'Star of Africa' was at long last in the ascendant. And I./JG 27's imminent re-equipment with the Bf 109F would transform the rise into one of meteoric proportions.

It was the arrival of Hauptmann Wolfgang Lippert's II. *Gruppe* at Ain-el-Gazala towards the end of September which permitted I./JG 27 to rotate back to Germany, one *Staffel* at a time, to exchange its war-weary

One pilot above all others who would make those skies his own was the now Leutnant Hans-Joachim Marseille (left). By October 1941 his score had risen to 25, for which he was awarded the German Cross in Gold, seen here being pinned on by his *Kommandeur* Hauptmann Eduard Neumann

Emils for brand new *Friedrichs*. The whole process would take well over a month.

Assuming the mantle of I. *Gruppe*, II./JG 27 soon got into its African stride. On 3 October the unit claimed a trio of Hurricanes just across the Egyptian border. Forty-eight hours later another pair went down, and on 6 October it was three more Hurricanes and a brace of Tomahawks. Just like I./JG 27, II. *Gruppe* also had its established *Experten*, and those who were still on the way up. Of these first ten kills in North Africa, three each

By the autumn of 1941 I. *Gruppe* had at long last been joined in the desert by II./JG 27, newly re-equipped in Germany with tan-camouflaged Bf 109F-4/trops. One such machine, 5. *Staffel's* 'Black 9', is here being refuelled alongside a somewhat rudimentary sandbagged blast-pen – still the only protection Ain-el-Gazala had to offer after more than seven months as the Luftwaffe's major fighter base in North Africa

Future *Experte* and Knight's Cross winner Oberfeldwebel Otto Schulz pictured in the cockpit of an F-4/trop of the *Gruppenstab* II./JG 27. Note that in addition to the *Gruppe's* 'Berlin bear' crest on the engine cowling, the machines of the *Stabsschwarm* also carried their own emblem beneath the windscreen – a surprised-looking lion with a sticking plaster already judiciously placed on the very spot another bullet was about to hit. Known among the *Gruppe* as '*verpflasterter Albion*' ('plastered Albion'), a variation of this badge featured a Union Jack flying from the lion's tail

71

Shot down behind Allied lines after claiming his 25th, and final, victory (a Hurricane east of Bir Hacheim on 23 November), Hauptmann Wolfgang Lippert, *Gruppenkommandeur* of II./JG 27, later died in a Cairo hospital from injuries he had received baling out of his doomed Bf 109

had been credited to Oberleutnant Gustav Rödel, the Knight's Cross-wearing *Kapitän* of 4./JG 27, and to one of the more promising NCO pilots of his *Staffel*, Oberfeldwebel Otto Schulz. This took their scores to 24 and 12 respectively.

But II./JG 27 would inevitably suffer its share of casualties too. And the first combat fatality was 5. *Staffel's* Leutnant Gustav-Adolf Langanke, shot down by return fire from a formation of SAAF Marylands he was attacking near Sidi Omar on 7 October.

It was Otto Schulz who brought down a Bristol Bombay near Ain-el-Gazala on the morning of 27 November, taking off, claiming his victim, and landing again all in the space of just three minutes! Only a handful of these elderly twin-engined transports would appear on JG 27's African scoresheets – twice with some significance. On this occasion the No 216 Sqn machine was one of five carrying troops of the embryonic Special Air Service (SAS) on their first ever large-scale raid behind enemy lines. Their objective was to destroy the aircraft dispersed on the five Luftwaffe airfields in the Gazala-Tmimi area as the prelude to a major British offensive scheduled to be launched the following day.

In the event, the SAS operation was 'not merely a failure, it was a debacle'. But the offensive opened on 18 November as planned. Intended to relieve Tobruk and drive Rommel's forces out of Cyrenaica (the eastern half of Libya), Operation *Crusader* would achieve both its aims.

Even nature lent a hand. Heavy rainstorms during the night of 17/18 November had turned the Gazala airfields into quagmires of mud, making it extremely difficult for the Bf 109s to operate. But an improvement in conditions soon led to fierce clashes between the opposing fighter forces. On 22 November II./JG 27 claimed at least ten Tomahawks, plus three Blenheims, in a series of engagements to the south of Tobruk. It lost four of its own machines, with two pilots being wounded. One, Leutnant Karl Scheppa of the *Stabsschwarm*, would be killed the following day when a bomb hit the Italian field hospital to which he had been taken.

Two of 22 November's Tomahawks had been downed by *Gruppenkommandeur* Hauptmann Wolfgang Lippert. Twenty-four hours later he added a Hurricane, but then his own machine was severely damaged. In baling out behind the British lines, he struck the tailplane and broke both his legs. At first the fractures appeared uncomplicated. After admittance to a Cairo hospital, however, it was discovered that gangrene had set in. Lippert refused the double amputation which offered the only chance of saving his life. In the end he relented, although by then it was too late. The operation was carried out on 3 December, but he died of a massive embolism only minutes after completion of the surgery. Wolfgang Lippert was buried by the British with full military honours.

Meanwhile, 1./JG 27 had returned to the fray in its new *Friedrichs*. The *Staffel's* first victory, a Tomahawk claimed on 12 November, had been a shared kill which, uncommon in the *Jagdwaffe*, had been credited to the unit as a whole. 1./JG 27 too had been involved in the heavy fighting of 22 and 23 November, the unit's total for the two days being 14 enemy aircraft destroyed, exactly half of them falling to *Staffelkapitän* Wolfgang Redlich. The *Staffel* lost two of its own NCOs shot down and captured.

By the end of the first week of December 3./JG 27 was also back in action – an event which Leutnant Hans-Joachim Marseille had duly

marked by claiming four Hurricanes in three days. This raised his total to 29, and brought him level with his *Staffelkapitän*, Oberleutnant Gerhard Homuth. In a spirit of friendly rivalry, the race between the two was now on. Of the *Gruppe's* two other top scorers, Wolfgang Redlich was still in the lead with 36. But on 5 December, the day his latest victim had gone down south of Bir-el-Gobi, he received a posting to the office of the General Staff. His replacement at the head of 1. *Staffel*, Oberleutnant Ludwig Franzisket, was currently standing at 24.

Such individual successes in the air were not enough to halt the dangers developing on the desert floor below. After a shaky start, Operation *Crusader* was by now gathering momentum. The Luftwaffe's forward airfields around Gambut had already been captured. And on 7 December 1941 – the day the world learned of the Japanese attack on Pearl Harbour – the long siege of Tobruk was finally lifted. This posed a direct threat to the Gazala complex, the next objective in the path of the advancing British armour. I. and II./JG 27 were forced to vacate their base on that same 7 December. The nearly eight months which I. *Gruppe* had spent at Ain-el-Gazala would be the longest deployment at any one field throughout JG 27's entire time in North Africa.

The *Gruppen's* first step on the long withdrawal back across Cyrenaica was but a short hop from Gazala. Tmimi, where it would remain for only five days, had witnessed III./JG 27's arrival from Germany just 24 hours earlier on 6 December. And when all three *Gruppen* were joined there by Oberstleutnant Bernhard Woldenga's *Stab* on 10 December, it meant that, for the first time since the Battle of Britain, the complete *Geschwader* was once again operating as a single entity – albeit in the midst of a general retreat!

For JG 27's *Friedrichs*, it was very much a fighting retreat. On the day of the *Geschwaderstab's* arrival in North Africa, the desert-wise I. *Gruppe* was up in force. Hans-Joachim Marseille added another Tomahawk to his lengthening list, while Hauptmann Erich Gerlitz's 2. *Staffel* downed all but one of a group of six unescorted SAAF Bostons. But I./JG 27 was

By November 1941 Hauptmann Redlich's 1. *Staffel* **had also completed conversion on to the F-4/trop. Here, a mechanic clutching the starting handle hastens away before the sand starts to fly as the pilot of 'White 2' guns his engine**

With the Allies' *Crusader* offensive in full swing, the bulk of the *Geschwader* had retired to Martuba by mid-December. Only just arrived in Africa, *Kommodore* Oberstleutnant Bernhard Woldenga (in fur-lined jacket) confers with General Erwin Rommel (in peaked cap and scarf) as they study situation maps on the bonnet of the latter's staff car

about to lose its two most successful NCO pilots under circumstances that were more than just unfortunate.

On 13 December Oberfeldwebel Albert Espenlaub of 1. *Staffel*, who had scored 11 of his 14 victories in the last month alone, was bested in combat near El Adem. He managed to belly-land his 'White 11' and was taken prisoner, only to be shot later in the day while attempting to escape from his captors. Less easy to explain and condone is the loss of 2. *Staffel*'s Oberfeldwebel Hermann Förster the following day. Förster's 13th, and last, kill had been one of the South African Bostons. Now, in a dogfight with Australian Tomahawks over recently abandoned Tmimi, his machine was hit and he was forced to bale out. He was fired upon and killed in his parachute.

By this time III./JG 27 had opened its desert account too. Unsurprisingly, perhaps, it was the *Geschwader*'s most successful pilot, and sole Oak

Curious Allied troops gather round Oberfeldwebel Espenlaub's 'White 11' after its forced landing near El Adem on 13 December. Quickly taken prisoner, Espenlaub was shot while making a break for freedom later that same day. By the time this photograph was taken a souvenir hunter had apparently already been at work hacking the 14 kill bars out of the rudder

While it was the pilots who undoubtedly faced the greatest dangers, a thought should be spared for the groundcrews whose daily lot it was – often under the most difficult and primitive of conditions – to keep the aircraft flying. Here, armourers of 3. *Staffel* (note oxygen cylinder marked 3. St. at right) check belts of 20 mm ammunition. The inscription on the jerricans in the foreground indicates that they contain machine gun lubricating oil

Leaves wearer, who had been responsible for its first two Allied fighters brought down near Tmimi on 12 December. These took Oberleutnant Erbo *Graf* von Kageneck's overall total to 67. But experience gained in Russia did not guarantee immunity in North Africa, and on 24 December it was von Kageneck who was at the receiving end of a burst from a No 94 Sqn Hurricane over Agedabia.

Although seriously wounded in the stomach, he reportedly managed to nurse his crippled fighter back the 46 miles (75 km) to the *Gruppe's* then base at Magrun and pull off an emergency landing. He was immediately evacuated, first to a hospital in Athens, and then to another in Naples where, despite intensive care, he died from his injuries on 12 January 1942.

By the final week of 1941 JG 27 had completed its withdrawal across Cyrenaica. The whole *Geschwader* was now gathered on landing grounds

Other tasks included the recovery of aircraft forced-landed in the desert. Again, these are men of 3. *Staffel* carefully dismantling 'Yellow 11' for transport back to base by truck

around the Arco Philaenorum. This was a grandiose arch, spanning the coast road, which had been erected by Mussolini to mark the dividing line between the two provinces of his Libyan empire: Cyrenaica to the east, Tripolitania to the west.

Having had to abandon and blow up a number of their machines on almost every one of the half-dozen or so airfields they had occupied, however briefly, during the recent retreat, the *Gruppen* were in something of a sorry state. But although bloody, they were unbowed. On the morning of 25 December Major Neumann, *Kommandeur* of I./JG 27, summoned the *Kapitän* of his 1. *Staffel*, Oberleutnant Ludwig Franzisket.

'We've got just four serviceable '109s left, "Ziskus". Fly up and down the coast road at medium height so that the ground troops can get to see a few German aircraft for Christmas at least.'

Oberleutnant Franzisket did as he was bid, but the effect was the very opposite to that intended. The traffic along Rommel's one major supply route had been subjected to Allied fighter-bomber attacks too many times in the past. As soon as the four aircraft were spotted approaching, every vehicle screeched to a halt as its occupants dived for cover at the side of the road. The end came as the Bf 109s circled above an Italian encampment near El Agheila. A well-placed 20 mm anti-aircraft round shattered Franzisket's canopy, sending a shower of splinters into his face and eyes. The wounds required specialist medical treatment, and 1. *Staffel* would not see their *Kapitän* again until March 1942.

Franzisket did not miss very much. By mid-January 1942 Operation *Crusader* had all but run its course. True, General Auchinleck's latest offensive had retaken nearly all the ground captured – and then lost – during General Wavell's pursuit of the Italian army across Cyrenaica a year earlier, but it had not engaged and destroyed the core of Rommel's forces. And it was the latter who now staged a surprise counter-attack.

On 29 January Rommel recaptured Benghazi (the fourth time the capital of Cyrenaica had changed hands in less than a year!), and by mid-February he was once again in possession of the airfields around Derna. Here the wily 'Desert Fox' would pause for the next three months.

Aerial activity during this period has since been described as 'limited'. But such a term is relative, and the high scorers of JG 27 were still taking their toll of enemy machines. In February the entire *Geschwader* moved back up to fields around Martuba, to the south-east of the Derna complex. Here, they would operate in conjunction with other Luftwaffe units stationed in the area, including the Stukas of I./StG 3, as the *NahkampfGruppe Martuba* (Martuba Close-support Group). Commanded by the *Kommodore* of JG 27, this *ad hoc* force was later rechristened the *Gefechtsverband* (Combat unit) *Woldenga*.

On 9 February 3./JG 27's Gerhard Homuth and Hans-Joachim Marseille had been level at 40 kills each. By month's end, however, the mercurial young Berliner was beginning to draw steadily ahead of his *Staffelkapitän*. Likewise, across at II. *Gruppe*, Otto Schulz – heaving downed five Tomahawks in ten minutes on 15 February – was also forging ahead of Gustav Rödel, *Kapitän* of 4. *Staffel*.

Leutnant Hans-Joachim Marseille and Oberfeldwebel Otto Schulz were each finally awarded the Knight's Cross on 22 February (for 50 and 44 victories respectively, the original '20-kill' benchmark having

On 21 February 1942 Leutnant Hans-Joachim Marseille got the two Kittyhawks which raised his total to 50 and earned him the Knight's Cross. Using gestures which will be immediately familiar to any member of the international fighter fraternity, he re-lives the action which took place shortly after noon to the west of Tobruk. *Staffelkapitän* Gerhard Homuth (right), who claimed the third of 3./JG 27's three Kittyhawks that day, listens impassively

Afterwards, Marseille watches as one of his groundcrew puts the finishing touches to the 50th victory bar on the primer red rudder of 'Yellow 14', Wk-Nr. 8693, at the *Geschwader's* Martuba base. Note the ten-bar template which allowed Marseille's increasingly frequent multiple kills to be recorded several at a time

Now the highest scoring pilot in the Mediterranean theatre, Leutnant Hans-Joachim had acquired celebrity status. Here he is introduced to Generalfeldmarschall Albert Kesselring, Luftwaffe AOC-in-C Mediterranean. Visible in this picture are, from left to right: Marseille's great friend Leutnant Hans-Arnold Stahlschmidt, Hauptmann Erich Gerlitz, Marseille (back to camera), Hauptmann Eduard Neumann, Kesselring and General Hans Geisler, AOC X. *Fliegerkorps*

Oberfeldwebel Otto Schulz of II. *Gruppe* ran Marseille a close second in the first half of 1942. The columns of smoke on the horizon are reportedly two of the five Kittyhawks which Schulz claimed in just ten minutes on the afternoon of 15 February 1942 after scrambling and chasing a group of Curtiss fighters (from Nos 94 and 112 Sqns) which had just strafed Martuba. This took his score to 44, which earned him the Knight's Cross alongside Marseille a week later

long gone by the board). For Marseille, it was the first significant official recognition (since the German Cross) of a burgeoning combat career that would see him wearing the Diamonds little more than six months later. For Schulz, it heralded the approaching end. Promoted to Oberleutnant and appointed II./JG 27's *Gruppen*-TO, he would be shot down and killed claiming his 51st victim, a Hurricane of No 274 Sqn, during a *freie Jagd* mission near Sidi Rezegh on 17 June.

On 23 March III./JG 27 had sent a small detachment to Crete. Based at Kastelli, the *Jagdkommando Kreta* would be slowly strengthened during the remaining months of the year as the eastern Mediterranean island grew in strategic significance. Commanded since near the close of their eastern front service by Hauptmann Erhard 'Jack' Braune (Max Dobislav having been appointed chief instructor at JFS 1 Werneuchen), III. *Gruppe*

was already beginning to see itself as the *Geschwader's* 'jack-of-all-trades' unit. This view was reinforced on 5 May when a fourth *Staffel* was added to its numbers. As its designation indicates, 10.(*Jabo*)/JG 27 was intended specifically for the fighter-bomber role.

On 18 April 'Edu' Neumann had organised the desert equivalent of a village fete to celebrate the anniversary of his *Gruppe's* first year in Africa. The bare expanse of Martuba was transformed by a colourful and motley collection of home-made stalls, sideshows and roundabouts. Guests from all the neighbouring German and Italian units were invited to the day-long festivities.

But for I. and II. *Gruppen's Experten* it was soon back to business as usual. On 20 May Oberleutnant Gustav Rödel was appointed *Kommandeur* of II./JG 27. He replaced Hauptmann Erich Gerlitz, who was to take over

A *Schwarm* of 5./JG 27 prepares for another hurried take-off. While the mechanic of the second machine ('Black 5') heaves on the starting handle, the pilot and groundcrew are still running for 'Black 10', the last in line. Nearest the camera, 'Black 4', with the II. *Gruppe* horizontal bar clearly visible on the white aft fuselage band, is probably a replacement aircraft, whereas the next two – with the white theatre band applied *over* the *Gruppe* marking – are more likely to be part of the original Döberitz contingent (see colour profile 16)

Wearing a kapok life-jacket, Hauptmann Eduard Neumann casts an anxious glance skywards – another surprise attack by the RAF, or is he counting his own pilots safely home after a hazardous overwater patrol?

Last seen on page 35, Eduard Neumann's ex-circus caravan also served I./JG 27 as a home-from-home in the desert. Emblazoned on the side was the name the *Gruppe* had given itself, *'Neumanns bunte Bühne'*, which translates roughly as 'Neumann's colourful cabaret'! Inside, the *Kommandeur* had a novel way of keeping track of his pilot's scores. Painted around the walls was a frieze of unclad native beauties, each with the name of a pilot above her head. For every victory a pilot scored, a palm-frond was added to his namesake's skirt. While some tyros had yet to amass enough kills to cover their young lady's modesty, 'Miss Marseille' must have felt positively overdressed!

III./JG 53, currently flying in to Martuba from Sicily to bolster the Luftwaffe's fighter presence in North Africa.

Two of the twelve Tomahawks and Kittyhawks claimed by II. *Gruppe* on 23 May were credited to the new *Kommandeur*, taking Rödel's total to 41. I. *Gruppe's* Oberleutnant Marseille was also regularly scoring daily doubles during this period. The two bombers he downed south-east of Tobruk on 23 May – victories number 63 and 64, claimed as Douglas DB-7s – were, in reality, a pair of No 223 Sqn Martin Baltimores flying that unit's first operational mission with the new type.

Three days later, on 26 May, Generaloberst Erwin Rommel launched the offensive which would take his *Afrika Korps* all the way to El Alamein. But first he had to smash a breach in the Allied lines, which now stretched from Gazala, on the coast, some 40 miles (65 km) inland down into the desert to the fortress of Bir Hacheim.

Released from their *Gefechtsverband Woldenga* duties, JG 27's fighters, reinforced by Gerlitz's III./JG 53, played a decisive part in the first six weeks

Another desert dwelling with more than its fair share of feminine charms on display was Marseille's own tent. Furnished with oriental rugs, and with armchairs made out of packing cases, its walls were hung with pictures from his many admirers – some recognisable as famous actresses. But what would Freud have made of that giant spider's web decoration in the corner?

General Rommel (to the right of the spinner) inspects one of the six Tomahawks of No 5 Sqn SAAF claimed by Oberleutnant Hans-Joachim Marseille west of the fortress of Bir Hacheim on 3 June 1942. These six victories raised Marseille's total to 75, and resulted in the award of the Oak Leaves three days later

of chaotic fighting that was the Battle of Gazala. On 3 June Hans-Joachim Marseille had his most successful day yet, destroying six Tomahawks in little more than ten minutes to the west of Bir Hacheim. Remarkably, he achieved this feat using just his two machine-guns, as his cannon having jammed after firing only ten rounds! These six Tomahawks of No 5 Sqn SAAF raised Marseille's total to 75, for which he was awarded the Oak Leaves on 6 June.

At the other end of the scale Oberstleutnant Bernhard Woldenga had not added to the four victories he had achieved in Russia. In fact, ill-health had prevented him from leading the *Geschwader* on operations over the desert. And on 10 June he was promoted to the first of the staff postings which would elevate him to the position of *Jafü Balkan*. He did, however, leave one tangible memento of his time as CO of the *Geschwader* – a *Stab* emblem based on the shield he had earlier designed for I./JG 1. The main difference was that the three small Bf 109 silhouettes were now pointing upwards. Critics of the original badge had expressed the view that the nose-down attitude of its three fighters suggested they were fleeing!

Woldenga's departure set in train a whole string of new appointments. Major Eduard Neumann replaced him as *Geschwaderkommodore*, Hauptmann Gerhard Homuth became *Kommandeur* of I./JG 27 and Oberleutnant Hans-Joachim Marseille took over as *Kapitän* of 3. *Staffel*.

The departure of the ailing Oberstleutnant Bernhard Woldenga led to Eduard Neumann's appointment to the command of JG 27. Here, the new *Kommodore* is pictured with his three *Gruppenkommandeure* (from left to right), Hauptmann Erhard Braune (III.), Hauptmann Gustav Rödel (II.), Major Neumann and Hauptmann Gerhard Homuth (I.), at Tmimi in June 1942

Exactly one week later, on 17 June, a brace each of Tomahawks and Hurricanes, claimed near Gambut, took Marseille's score to 99. He was exhausted and ready to call it a day but, encouraged by the other three members of his *Schwarm* – 'Come on, Jochen, now for the hundredth!' – he felt honour-bound to oblige.

A lone Hurricane shot down in flames into an anti-aircraft emplacement south of Gambut airfield made Hans-Joachim Marseille only the 11th Luftwaffe fighter pilot to reach a century – but the first to achieve this total against the western Allies alone!

He even found time to go into a steep climb three minutes after despatching the low-level Hurricane in order to add number 101 (a high-flying photo-reconnaissance Spitfire which, if identified correctly, was the first for the *Geschwader* since the Battle of Britain), before returning to the familiar surroundings of Ain-el-Gazala, which I./JG 27 had re-occupied just 24 hours earlier.

The following day, 18 June, Marseille departed in a Ju 52/3m for Berlin, where he was to be presented with the Swords to his Oak Leaves. He was delighted with the ceremonial of the occasion, but revelled even more in the rapturous welcome his hometown accorded him during his subsequent weeks' leave. It was the celebrities and stars whose attention he had once courted who were now falling over themselves to be seen in the company of the Reich's newest national hero.

Meanwhile, back in the desert things were happening fast. On 21 June the 'fortress' of Tobruk, which had withstood an eight-month siege the year before, had been taken within a matter of days. Seventy-two hours later the *Afrika Korps* crossed the Egyptian border in force. Rommel's Panzers did not stop until they bumped into the main Allied line of defence, the northern flank of which was anchored at a small halt on the coastal railway called El Alamein.

During this period 'Jack' Braune's somewhat overshadowed III. *Gruppe* were also achieving a number of successes. On 15 June Oberleutnant Hans-Joachim Heinecke – *Kapitän* of 9./JG 27, and recently posted in from JG 53 with 18 kills already to his credit – had claimed the *Geschwader's* first four-engined heavy bomber . . . a portent of things to come! The B-24 Liberator had been part of a small Anglo-American force searching for Italian naval units off the Egyptian coast.

Erhard 'Jack' Braune had become *Kommandeur* of III./JG 27 in October 1941 when the unit was still on the eastern front. But even later in North Africa the '*Gruppe* Braune' was not allowed to forget its East Prussian roots. As this sign along the Libyan coast road indicates, Königsberg is only 2999.9 kilometres away (via nearby 'New Jesau', presumably the *Gruppe's* name for the patch of sand in the desert where it was currently based)

The new *Kapitän* of 3./JG 27, cigarette in mouth, clowns at the wheel of a *Kübelwagen* (Volkswagen's answer to the jeep) laden to the springs with members of his *Staffel*. Although the open driver's door hides the evidence, this is almost certainly Marseille's own runabout, which he christened *OTTO* and adorned with paintings of desert lizards and the like (see picture on page 111)

Another of I. *Gruppe's* undeniable characters was Hans-Arnold Stahlschmidt, pictured here as an Oberfeldwebel serving with JG 27's *Ergänzungsstaffel* at Oldenburg prior to transfer to North Africa, where he would score all of his 59 victories. It is not known whether the shield beneath the windscreen – which appears to show an Iron Cross half-submerged in the sea, with a setting sun behind it – was the badge of the *Staffel*, or 'Fifi' Stahlschmidt's own tongue-in-cheek comment on his future prospects!

Another of Braune's newly-appointed *Staffelkapitäne*, Leutnant Werner Schroer of 8./JG 27 (ex-Adjutant of I. *Gruppe*), also began to make his presence felt. Taking over on 23 June with his score standing at 11, he would more than double this figure within a fortnight.

Between 24 and 26 June Major Neumann's *Stab* and all three *Gruppen* staged forward from their fields around Gazala and Tmimi, via Gambut, to gather briefly at Sidi Barrani. It was the first time their wheels had touched down on Egyptian soil – or should that be sand? In the next couple of weeks JG 27's fighters would move up closer still to the Alamein front, as both sides prepared for the decisive battle which neither could afford to lose. From early July until late October I. and II. *Gruppen* would operate primarily out of Quotaifiya, little more than 30 miles (50 km) from the frontline.

Throughout July Homuth and Rödel's pilots whittled away at the opposition. Their victims included nearly every operational type to be found in the Allied Air Forces' armoury – and possibly one that wasn't, for the 'Gladiator' claimed by 2. *Staffel's* Leutnant Hans-Arnold Stahlschmidt near El Daba on 7 July appears more likely, in retrospect, to have been an Italian CR.42! Unabashed, 'Fifi' Stahlschmidt brought down a trio of Hurricanes the next day, taking his score to 30, before adding a further 17 kills by mid-August to earn himself a Knight's Cross.

It was another imminent Knight's Cross winner, Feldwebel Günther Steinhausen of 1. *Staffel*, who was credited with JG 27's second B-24. One of six USAAF machines sent to attack an Axis convoy on 9 July, B-24D *Eager Beaver* went down into the sea in flames. The bomber was victory number 34 for Steinhausen. His total was standing at 40 when he himself crashed to his death during a dogfight south-east of El Alamein on 6 September. Promotion to Leutnant and award of the Knight's Cross were both posthumous.

Far removed from El Alamein, where he was shot down, Leutnant Friedrich Körner (right), a member of Stahlschmidt's 2./JG 27, stands in the snow with a group of fellow prisoners in a (Canadian?) PoW camp wearing the Knight's Cross awarded, and presented, to him after capture

Twenty-four hours after Steinhausen was posted missing, Leutnant Stahlschmidt, by then *Kapitän* of 2. *Staffel*, would be lost in similar circumstances, and in the same area. He, too, would be honoured posthumously, being awarded the Oak Leaves for his final total of 59 desert victories. Coincidentally, one Knight's Cross *had been* awarded on 6 September. It went to 2./JG 27's Leutnant Friedrich Körner, a 36-victory *Experte* who had also been shot down in combat near El Alamein two months earlier on 4 July, but who had survived to become a PoW.

July had also seen *Geschwader*-Adjutant Hauptmann Ernst Düllberg continue a tradition which had been started back in the days of the Battle of Britain and the Balkans by claiming the *Geschwaderstab's* one and only kill of the entire North African campaign – a Hurricane south-west of Alamein in the early evening of the 13th.

It was on 7 August that a *Schwarm* from 5./JG 27, led by Oberfeldwebel Emil Clade, chanced upon another of the occasional Bombay transports of No 216 Sqn. But this machine was not carrying SAS troops (who had long since taken to using jeeps for their forays behind Axis lines). It was instead on the daily flight from Heliopolis to pick up wounded from the front for transport back to hospital in Cairo.

At one forward landing ground, however, the Bombay's 18-year-old pilot, Sgt H E James, was ordered to wait for a special passenger. This turned out to be Lt Gen W H E Gott, who, only hours previously, had been appointed Commander of the 8th Army, and who now needed to get back to Cairo for an urgent meeting.

Rather than fly at the stipulated 50 ft (15 m) to escape the attentions of Axis fighters, the pilot elected to climb to 500 ft (150 m) on account of an overheating engine. It was his undoing. Clade's first pass forced the lumbering Bombay to crash-land in the desert to the south-east of Alexandria. Some of the crew and passengers attempted to escape from the still moving machine. All but one of those remaining inside, including Gott, were killed when Unteroffizier Bernd Schneider carried out a strafing run to finish off the stricken machine. Lt Gen Gott was the highest ranked British soldier to be killed by enemy fire in World War 2. His death led to the hurried appointment of a replacement commander for the 8th Army – a relative unknown named Bernard Law Montgomery.

The Bombay was 5. *Staffel*'s only claim for the fortnight between 4 and 19 August. Over the same period all that 6./JG 27 managed to bring down was a pair of Kittyhawks. But the remaining 4. *Staffel* of II. *Gruppe* – or, to be more precise, just one *Schwarm* of that *Staffel* – submitted claims during that time for no fewer than 59 Allied fighters destroyed! This huge discrepancy in numbers, and the lack of any witnesses other than the *Schwarm* members themselves, gave rise to grave suspicions. But rather than take the matter to higher authority, and possibly throw doubt and disrepute on the rest of the *Gruppe*, it was decided simply to break up the offending *Schwarm*. It should be noted that a full two months were to pass before the erstwhile *Schwarmführer* claimed his next victory, and that one of his NCO pilots disappeared over the Mediterranean on 19 August 'for reasons unknown' (some suggested he chose deliberately to dive into the sea rather than face accusations of making false claims and possible court-martial). The other two, however, went on to attain legitimate and respectable scores.

While tension may have been high at Quotaifiya, life for III./JG 27 at Quasaba during August was more hum-drum. Only three Kittyhawks were added to the *Gruppe*'s scoreboard, and much of the month was spent on coastal convoy patrol duties. 10.(*Jabo*) *Staffel*, which had carried out fighter-bomber raids on targets as far afield as Alexandria early in July, was now being employed against vehicle parks and gun emplacements closer to the front. And at the end of August the *Staffel* was withdrawn from III. *Gruppe*'s control altogether to become part of the autonomous *JaboGruppe Afrika*. Finally, 31 August also saw the loss of Oberleutnant Hermann Tangerding, *Kapitän* of 7. *Staffel*, who took a direct anti-aircraft hit during a Stuka escort mission south of El Alamein.

III. *Gruppe*'s woes were not echoed back at I./JG 27's Quotaifiya dispersals. And for good reason. Wearing his Swords, the *Kapitän* of 3. *Staffel* was back in Africa, and back in business. On that same 31 August Oberleutnant Marseille had claimed a couple of Hurricanes in the morning, likewise while escorting Stukas south-east of El Alamein, plus a single Spitfire in the early evening.

But it was the events of the following day which are still a source of no little controversy. Many, including RAF pilots who fought in the desert war, question the validity of Marseille's claims for the 17 Allied fighters he is reported to have shot down on 1 September (a total exceeded only by the world-record 18 achieved by Emil Lang on the eastern front – see *Osprey Aviation Elite 6 - Jagdgeschwader 54 'Grünherz'*). Post-war research has failed to identify all 17 of Marseille's alleged victims. It has proved,

Pictured here at Quotaifiya sporting the Swords which had been presented to him in Berlin, it was over the El Alamein front on 1 September that Oberleutnant Hans-Joachim Marseille claimed his still controversial 17 kills in a single day

however, that whereas he claimed all but one (a Spitfire) as Kittyhawks, at least half were in fact Hurricanes.

Although possibly two, and maybe even as many as four, of Marseille's opponents were not actually destroyed, the victories he did amass during his three sorties east of El Alamein on that 1 September make it without doubt the most successful day of his career.

Twenty-four hours later another five claims took Oberleutnant Marseille's score to 126, which won him the Diamonds. On this occasion there was to be no immediate summons to Berlin. And by the time the award was announced on 4 September his total had already risen to 132. A further dozen kills were added in the week that followed. Then, on 15 September, the sixth of seven enemy fighters credited to Marseille (all identified as 'P-46s', JG 27's erroneous designation for the Kittyhawk) gave him his 150th. He was only the third Luftwaffe pilot to reach this figure.

Although Marseille's 150 brought no further decorations (at the time there *was* nothing higher than the Diamonds), it did result in his immediate promotion to Hauptmann. Still three months short of his 23rd birthday, Hans-Joachim Marseille had become the youngest Hauptmann in the Luftwaffe.

He was also by far the highest scorer against the western Allies. But seven more victories were still to be added. They were claimed on 26 September, the 158th, and last of all – a Spitfire – going down near El Hamman, another halt on the coastal railway two stops to the east of El Alamein.

But Nemesis was already at hand. The two missions of 26 September had both been flown in new Bf 109G-2/trops. The first six of these machines, which were to replace the *Gruppe's* trusty *Friedrichs*, had just been delivered, and all had been allocated to Hauptmann Marseille's 3. *Staffel*. One of them, *Gustav* Wk-Nr. 14256, was to bring about the unthinkable, and something which 158 aerial opponents had signally failed to accomplish – the death of Hans-Joachim Marseille.

On 30 September Marseille was leading his *Schwarm* on yet another *freie Jagd* behind the Alamein front when his engine began to burn. Within seconds the cockpit was full of smoke. Choking on the fumes and unable to

The first day of September 1942 had undoubtedly been the most successful of Marseille's entire career. But the last day of the same month would bring that career to a tragic end. A member of JG 27 gazes in apparent disbelief at the almost unrecognisable remains of Bf 109G-2/trop Wk-Nr. 14256, whose defective engine was responsible for the death of the 'Star of Africa'

Hauptmann Hans-Joachim Marseille's remains lay 'in state' in the back of a truck, flanked by an honour guard, before burial at Derna, where Generalfeldmarschall Kesselring delivered an emotional funeral oration

Portrait of a national hero. The picture signed and sent by Luftwaffe C-in-C Hermann Göring to Frau Charlotte Marseille. The inscription below reads, 'In memory of the most outstanding fighter pilot in the world! To the mother of our immortal Hauptmann Marseille. Hermann Göring. Reichsmarschall'

see, Marseille sought desperately to get back to the German lines guided by instructions over the R/T from his wingman, Oberleutnant Jost Schlang. Nine minutes after the fire had first broken out, the *Gustav* – on its first operational flight – suddenly flipped onto its back and plunged earthwards in a steep dive. Marseille managed to extricate himself, but his body slammed heavily against the tailplane. Parachute unopened, his lifeless form crashed to the desert floor near the tiny white mosque of Sidi Abd el Rahman, just to the rear of Rommel's forward minefield defences.

Geschwaderkommodore Major Eduard Neumann, who had once prophesied that he would make a fighter pilot out of the precocious young Berliner, issued an Order of the Day. It ended with these sentences;

'His successes against our toughest aerial opponents, the English, are unique. We can be happy and proud to have counted him as one of us. There are no words eloquent enough to convey what his loss means to us. He leaves behind an obligation for us to follow his lead, both as a human being and as a soldier. His spirit will remain an example to the *Geschwader* for ever.'

The pilots of 3. *Staffel* had their own way of mourning the loss of their 'Jochen'. They shared a fig cake and listened to his favourite tune, 'Rumba Azul', on the wind-up gramophone.

Forty-eight hours later, whether at the instigation of a particularly understanding member of the Higher Command, or simply as a result of operational expediency, I./JG 27 was offered a complete change of scenery. Staging via the heel of Italy, where it converted fully on to the Bf 109G-2/trop, the *Gruppe* transferred to Sicily to take part in the renewed air offensive against Malta. During its near three-week stay at Pacino, the unit had accounted for seven RAF Spitfires. But two pilots had been lost, one to unknown causes and the other crashing into the sea due to yet another engine failure.

By this time III./JG 27 had moved forward from Quasaba to Turbiya, closer to the Alamein front. But the *Gruppe's* morale was at a low ebb.

Successes were still hard to come by, and its pilots were fed up of being treated as the *Geschwader's* 'poor relations'. This had only been heightened when they were handed II./JG 27's war-weary *Friedrichs*, which they would continue to fly while the other two *Gruppen* converted to the Bf 109G – although given the latter model's early accident rate, this may have been a blessing in disguise!

Knowing of his imminent promotion to the staff of XI. *Fliegerkorps*, and also fully aware of his *Gruppe's* problems, it is reported that 'Jack' Braune had even suggested that Hans-Joachim Marseille should be appointed his successor in an attempt to inject some spirit into the unit. Whether this proposal was given serious consideration is not known. But the 'Star of Africa' was no more. And when Hauptmann Erhard Braune departed on 11 October, his replacement was ex-*Geschwader*-Adjutant Hauptmann Ernst Düllberg.

One bright spot in III./JG 27's sea of woes was provided by Leutnant Werner Schroer. Although not in the same league as Marseille, the *Kapitän* of 8. *Staffel* had continued to score steadily. On 20 October his 49th kill earned him the Knight's Cross. Less than 72 hours later, on the morning of 23 October, a pair of 'P-46s' east of El Alamein took his tally to 51.

But III. *Gruppe's* troubles, imagined or otherwise, were to be overwhelmed by a far greater disaster which was to affect not just JG 27, but the whole of the Axis forces in North Africa. For later that same evening 882 artillery pieces opened fire as one. Night turned into day. Gen Montgomery had begun the Battle of El Alamein.

I./JG 27 was rushed back from Sicily, but not even this most experienced of desert *Jagdgruppen* could do anything to influence events on the ground now. By 3 November it had claimed its final 13 victories over Egypt, two of

The death of Marseille heralded the beginning of the end for JG 27 in North Africa, for soon afterwards it was to embark upon the retreat across Cyrenaica. But there were still victories to be achieved and losses to be suffered, such as III. *Gruppe's* 'White 7' pictured here. Pilot Leutnant Helmuth Fenzl was taken prisoner after coming down behind Allied lines on 26 October 1942. Yet, oddly, this photograph, of German origin, show a truck (in fact, a captured British Bedford) clearly bearing German markings – or is that perhaps a red cross – at the crash site. Was this area subsequently retaken in a local counter-attack?

which had been credited to *Kommandeur* Hauptmann Gerhard Homuth, raising his total to 61.

The top scorers of all three *Gruppen* were remarkably level at this stage. A trio of P-40s downed over the battlefield on the opening morning of Montgomery's offensive had been numbers 63-65 for Hauptmann Gustav Rödel, *Kommandeur* of II./JG 27. Further to the west, one of a pair of B-24s claimed by III. *Gruppe* on 4 November provided the now Oberleutnant Werner Schroer with his 60th.

4 November was the day British and Commonwealth forces broke through the Axis front at El Alamein. Rommel's great retreat had begun. By 12 November the last German and Italian troops had been chased out of Egypt. For the British the 'Third Benghazi Stakes' were off and running. And this time it was to be a one-way race. This latest advance across Cyrenaica would not be driven back. It would continue through the Arco Philaenorum (inevitably, 'Marble Arch' to the passing British), across Tripolitania and only end with the total surrender of all Axis forces in Tunisia.

'Edu' Neumann's JG 27 was spared this final ignominy. After retiring to fields in western Cyrenaica, and having been forced to abandon many of their machines on the way, Stab, I. and III. *Gruppen* handed over most of their remaining Bf 109s to JG 77. They were then evacuated from North Africa on 12 November.

II./JG 27 was to remain nearly a month longer before it too passed its aircraft over to JG 77 and finally departed. During that time, based latterly at Merduma, just across the provincial border in Tripolitania, it lost three pilots killed but claimed six Allied fighters destroyed. The last one of all, fittingly a Kittyhawk, went to a tyro of 6. *Staffel* (Leutnant Hans Lewes – it was his first victory) during the *Gruppe's* final sortie on the morning of 6 December.

Jagdgeschwader 27's 20-month African odyssey was over.

Puzzle picture No 2 – often illustrated, and long thought to be the aircraft of 'Edu' Neumann's successor, Gustav Rödel, when *Kommodore* of JG 27 in Sicily in the spring of 1943, this photograph of the distinctively-marked 'White Triple Chevron 4', taken from the port side, shows a background terrain – billiard-table flat and dotted with camel-thorn scrub – much more reminiscent of North Africa. It is now believed that this machine is one belonging to the *Geschwaderstab* of JG 77 which was abandoned in Tripolitania in January 1943 – but proof positive has yet to be established

THE MEDITERRANEAN, AEGEAN AND BALKANS

The withdrawal from North Africa brought a fresh parting of the ways for the *Geschwader*. It also heralded the end of its uniquely 'desert' character. But before JG 27 became just another cog in the all-encompassing Defence of the Reich organisation, it still had important roles to perform in the Mediterranean and south-east European theatres.

After a period of much needed rest and recuperation in the homeland, *Stab* and II. *Gruppe* staged back down the length of Italy to Sicily late in February 1943. Major Neumann's *Geschwaderstab*, still flying F-4/trops, took up residence at San Pietro, some 20 miles (32 km) inland from Sicily's southern coast. II./JG 27, equipped with a mix of G-4s and G-6s, and with many new pilots now making up its depleted numbers, began operating out of Trapani on the north-western corner of the island, but also deployed detachments on occasion to San Pietro.

The unit's tasks were twofold: to continue the campaign against Malta, and to protect the Axis supply convoys – both sea and air – transporting reinforcements to Tunisia.

Malta was no longer the embattled Allied outpost of earlier years. Its fighter and bomber squadrons were now taking the war to Sicily's shores, and this fact was well illustrated on 3 March, when 5. *Staffel* claimed six Spitfires without loss – three south of San Pietro in the morning, and another trio off Malta shortly after midday.

Four of the RAF fighters (two on each sortie) had fallen to Feldwebel Bernd Schneider. This quartet took Schneider's total to 18. But his promising career was soon to be cut short. Promoted to Leutnant and appointed *Gruppen*-Adjutant, he scored his 23rd, and final, victory, (a USAAF P-38) on 29 April, only to be shot down himself moments later.

Both the 82nd FG Lightning and Schneider's 'Yellow 3' went into the sea to the west of Sicily. By this time II./JG 27's efforts were focused almost entirely upon the protection of the supply convoys running the 100-mile (160-km) gauntlet of the Mediterranean 'narrows' between Sicily and Tunisia, where the remains of the *Afrika Korps* were now hemmed in, their backs to the sea, facing the combined might of the Allied 1st and 8th Armies. But Hitler's determination to retain a toehold in North Africa was more than matched by that of the Allies, who were intent on severing his fragile lines of supply.

A special air offensive, Operation *Flax*, had been launched on 5 April specifically to cut off the flow of reinforcements and supplies being despatched by sea and air from Axis bases in Sicily and southern Italy. The first victim of *Flax* was a formation of Ju 52/3ms approaching Tunis on the opening morning. Caught by P-38s, 13 of the 31 transports were shot down, together with the two escorting *Gustavs* of 5./JG 27.

Nor was *Flax* restricted solely to attacking the convoys while en route. The offensive also included bombing raids by USAAF 'heavies' on their ports and airfields of departure and arrival. By the day's end *Flax* had accounted for a total of 26 transport aircraft destroyed (11 on the ground) and a further 65 damaged. II./JG 27's claims for that 5 April were a more modest six. But the identities of their victims – three B-17s and three P-38s – were significant, for throughout the remaining months of the war the majority of JG 27's opponents would be American.

One of 5 April's claimants (for a P-38) had been future Knight's Cross recipient Leutnant Willy Kientsch of 6. *Staffel*. In fact, by adding 25 kills to the 17 he had previously scored in the desert, Kientsch would emerge as the *Gruppe's* most successful pilot of the Sicilian campaign.

But individual successes counted for little against the overwhelming, and ever increasing, weight of Allied air superiority. Axis supply ships continued to be sunk, and transport aeroplanes shot out of the sky, and there was little II./JG 27 could do to prevent it. On the evening of 18 April less than a dozen of the *Gruppe's Gustavs* formed the main body of the escort for a force of 65 Ju 52/3ms departing Tunis for the return flight to Sicily. Flying in 'three enormous vics', the transports hugged the wave-tops as they set out on their perilous journey. They were little more than six miles (ten kilometres) out over the Mediterranean when they were spotted by patrolling Allied fighters.

What ensued has gone down in aviation history as the 'Palm Sunday Massacre' – 24 of the Junkers were shot into the sea, while a further 35 managed to stagger back to crash-land along the Tunisian coastline. Just six made it safely to Sicily! II./JG 27's sole contribution was the claiming of a single Spitfire by 6. *Staffel's* Feldwebel Albin Dorfer.

No doubt at all that this is Sicily, as the looming backdrop presence of the 2500-ft (750-m) Monte Erice identifies this as Trapani airfield on the north-western tip of the island. The group in the foreground are the pilots and groundcrew of 6./JG 27, with *Staffelkapitän* and future Knight's Cross winner Leutnant Willy Kientsch in the centre of the front row, hands clasped below his belt buckle. The photograph was taken in June 1943

Four days later the same *Staffel* lost two pilots when seven Bf 109s tried to protect 14 Me 323 *Gigants* – huge six-engined transports developed from the earlier Me 321 glider – against attack by a reported 80(!) Allied P-40s and Spitfires off Tunisia. Every one of the wood and canvas-clad behemoths was destroyed, while II./JG 27 managed to account for just three of their assailants.

It was on this same 22 April 1943 that Oberstleutnant Eduard Neumann relinquished command of the *Geschwader* to join the staff of the *General der Jagdflieger*. His successor was the *Kommandeur* of II./JG 27, Major Gustav Rödel. Unlike the two previous *Kommodoren*, Rödel was a firm believer in personal leadership not just on the ground, but in the air as well. He would be responsible for all five of the victories – two B-17s and three P-38s – credited to the *Stab* during its last two months in Sicily.

Gustav Rödel's place at the head of II. *Gruppe* was in turn filled by bringing in Hauptmann Werner Schroer, the experienced *Kapitän* of 8. *Staffel*. Schroer arrived in Sicily with 63 kills already under his belt. Starting with a couple of P-38s claimed south of the island on 29 April, Schroer's overall total would climb to 85 by the time the *Gruppe* withdrew to Germany in July. This made him second only to Willy Kientsch – himself now *Kapitän* of 6. *Staffel* – in terms of enemy aircraft destroyed during II./JG 27's final phase in the Mediterranean.

By the end of April the situation of the Axis forces bottled up around Cape Bon, the north-easternmost tip of Tunisia, had deteriorated to one of imminent collapse. II./JG 27 had sent a small *Kommando* back to North Africa during the last week of the month, but its ground-support missions along the rim of the *Afrika Korps'* shrinking perimeter achieved little, and it were soon recalled to Sicily. The last Axis troops in Tunisia surrendered two weeks later, and by then Allied air forces – now unified under a single Mediterranean Air Command – had already turned their attention towards the 'soft underbelly' of Europe.

And nowhere was this underbelly arguably softer, or more vulnerable, than Sicily. Throughout May the island's fighter airfields suffered a series of devastating heavy bomber raids. A lot of damage was caused, but II./JG 27 countered by bringing down more than 20 of the four-engined 'heavies', plus an almost equal number of their escorting P-38s, during the course of the month. Now fighting over 'home' territory, the *Gruppe's* casualties were confined to one pilot killed and another missing, although several others were forced to bale out wounded.

With the whole of the North African coastline now in Allied hands, it was obvious that the next stage of the Anglo-American offensive would involve an invasion of southern Europe. But less obvious was exactly where such an operation would be aimed – at Sicily, and thence up the leg of Italy, or via the Aegean islands northwards into Greece and the Balkans?

A hefty clue was provided by the intense aerial bombardment of Pantelleria. This rocky island, situated almost exactly midway between Sicily and Tunisia, was Italy's 'Malta'. It could, and should, have played a major part in Mediterranean air operations. But it never attained the renown of its George Cross counterpart. Indeed, its main claim to fame is that its surrender was brought about by air power alone.

Heavy round-the-clock bombing of Pantelleria commenced on 5 June. The crescendo of raids reached their climax five days later when it was

Once JG 27 had retired from North Africa to airfields on the northern shores of the Mediterranean, the dangers of ground-strafing by fighters of the Desert Air Force gave way to the threat of bombing raids by US four-engined 'heavies'. As groundcrew push a II. *Gruppe Gustav* to safety, smoke billows from wreckage on the far side of the field. Sources have variously identified this as coming from a crashed B-24 or burning Bf 109s – the latter seems more likely

reported that 'the air assault became so intense that aeroplanes arriving over the target area had to queue up before going in to bomb'.

II./JG 27's sole bomber victim on that 10 June was a twin-engined *Boston*. It was claimed by *Kommandeur* Hauptmann Werner Schroer, together with a pair of 'P-46s' brought down off the south coast of Sicily. The only other successes were a trio of Spitfires destroyed near Pantelleria, two falling to Leutnant Willy Kientsch. But the *Gruppe* paid a heavy price – the heaviest of their entire Sicilian sojourn, in fact. Ten of its *Gustavs* were shot down into the sea, with only one pilot surviving. Willy Kientsch's 6. *Staffel* was hardest hit with six losses. 4. *Staffel* reported three pilots missing. 5./JG 27's single fatality was Leutnant Hans Lewes, who had scored the *Geschwader's* last desert kill six months previously, and who had added just two more since.

Allied aircraft approaching Pantelleria on 11 June reported surrender signs being displayed. Nothing now stood in the way of a seaborne invasion of Sicily. But, as in North Africa, II./JG 27 would escape the closing stages of this next Allied offensive. Other *Jagdgruppen* – evacuees from the Tunisian debacle – were beginning to arrive in Sicily. And on 20 June Hauptmann Werner Schroer and his pilots were ordered to fly out to Lecce on the heel of Italy.

The return to mainland Europe brought scant relief for the depleted *Gruppe*. US heavy bombers were already biting deeper into the 'soft underbelly'. High on their list of priority targets were the Axis airfields, including Lecce. During one such raid, on 2 July, II./JG 27 achieved a rare success by claiming six out of a formation of 22 unescorted B-24s.

Eight days later Anglo-American forces landed on Sicily. On the first afternoon of the invasion II./JG 27, equipped with long-range tanks, attacked the British landing beaches around Syracuse and was able to bring down three Spitfires. Next day, 11 July, it was back in action over Italy, being credited with two B-24s south of Crotone.

On 12 July a small detachment returned to Sicily to operate alongside JG 53. It claimed three more Spitfires during its short stay, but had to abandon three unserviceable Bf 109s when ordered back to Italy 72 hours later. With Lecce rendered untenable by the recent bombing, the *Gruppe* was now based at San Vito dei Normanni, north of Brindisi.

It was from here, on 16 July, that II./JG 27 fought the last major engagement of its Mediterranean campaign. In less than 30 minutes its pilots reportedly shot down another six B-24s – part of a force attacking the airfield at Bari. They lost one of their own, plus had another seriously wounded. Despite his injuries, Hauptmann Ernst Börngen, *Kapitän* of 5. *Staffel*, was able to crash-land back at San Vito.

Although the days that followed would bring five more victories (three 'heavies' and a pair of Spitfires) and result in four more losses (including Börngen's immediate successor at the head of 5./JG 27), the *Gruppe's* time in Italy was rapidly drawing to a close. On 28 July II./JG 27 was ordered to hand over its last 17 serviceable *Gustavs* to other units – primarily JG 53 – and return by rail to the homeland for a short period of rest and re-equipment.

Major Gustav Rödel's *Geschwaderstab*, which had been based alongside II. *Gruppe* at Lecce during the latter part of June, had also departed Italy in July. It had not headed northwards for Germany, however, but eastwards to Kalamaki, in Greece, where Rödel, sporting his newly-awarded Oak Leaves, was to assume direct control of two of other *Gruppen* of his by now far-flung *Geschwader* – the African veterans of III./JG 27, currently re-equipping, and the recently activated IV./JG 27.

When III. *Gruppe* had left Libya back in November 1942, its journey had taken the unit to Kastelli, on the island of Crete. Here, it would remain for almost four months, ostensibly 'resting' but, at the same time, guarding the approaches to Greece and the Aegean. During the early weeks of 1943, 8./JG 27 had been detached to Rhodes, and it was

The end in the desert did not mean the end of desert-camouflaged machines for III./JG 27. Fully re-equipped with yet more *Friedrichs* after their arrival in Crete late in 1942, at least one aircraft – 'Black 11' pictured here – still wore the old tan-*hellblau* colour scheme. It had presumably suffered major damage earlier in its career and had just been returned to service after lengthy repairs. Note the non-standard fuselage cross (see colour profile 20) and what appears to be a replacement starboard wing in temperate grey-green camouflage

From its base on Rhodes 8./JG 27 patrolled the entrance to the Aegean. This G-2/trop is 'Red 1', the machine of *Staffelkapitän* Oberleutnant Werner Schroer. Just visible on the rudder are at least 60 victory bars, Schroer's 61 kills in North Africa having made him the second most successful desert *Experte* after Marseille. The two 'Beauforts' claimed off Scarpanto on 11 February 1943 were numbers 62 and 63

Staffelkapitän Oberleutnant Werner Schroer who had claimed the *Gruppe's* first two victories of the new year.

Schroer downed the two machines, which he identified as Beauforts, off the island of Scarpanto on 11 February. It now seems more likely, however, that these were the pair of Marauders reported missing by No 14 Sqn RAF on 15 February. The mis-identification may be

Italian pilots of the *Regia Aeronatica's* 154° *Gruppo* are given a closer look at Werner Schroer's 'Red 1' on Rhodes in March. But this attempt to cement friendly relations with their Axis partners and neighbours on the island would founder six months later with Italy's surrender to the Allies. The 8./JG 27 NCO standing on the wing is Feldwebel Alfred Stückler . . .

. . . who is pictured here (left) overseeing the painting of a fourth victory bar on the rudder of his aircraft to mark the shooting down of a RAF Beaufighter on 13 June

attributed to the Marauder's being a relatively new and unfamiliar type – and the confusion in dates to the fact that Schroer was flying back to Crete at the time, and then home on leave to get married – perhaps he had other things on his mind!

In March, while the situation remained quiet in the eastern Mediterranean, 7. and 9. *Staffeln* were ordered to Bari, in Italy, to convert on to the Bf 109G. III./JG 27 was at last about to bid farewell to its long-serving *Friedrichs*. Once conversion was complete, the two *Staffeln* were then sent to San Pietro, on Sicily, to take part in the operations against Malta. These resulted in III./JG 27's next two kills – a brace of Spitfires on 12 April credited to the *Kapitän* of 7. *Staffel*, Oberleutnant Günther Hannak, who was a 41-victory Knight's Cross-wearer recently transferred in from JG 77. They were Hannak's only kills with his new unit. Less than a month later, on 5 May, engine trouble forced him down over Malta, and into captivity.

After briefly participating in convoy-escort duties to Tunisia, which cost them six of their new *Gustavs*, 7. and 9. *Staffeln* headed back east in late May to rejoin 8./JG 27 at the *Gruppe's* new base on the Greek mainland at Tanagra, north-west of Athens. With Hauptmann Werner Schroer having in the meantime been appointed *Kommandeur* of II./JG 27, 8. *Staffel* was now headed by Oberleutnant Dietrich Boesler.

But even greater changes were afoot as plans for the creation of an entirely new *Gruppe* were finalised. Using the same pre-war *Mutter-Tochterverband* method which had seen I./JG 1 bring I./JG 21 into being, so now III./JG 27 (the descendants of that original I./JG 1) was mainly instrumental in the activation of IV./JG 27. One whole *Staffel*, Boesler's 8., was transferred to the new *Gruppe's* base at Kalamaki, where it was redesignated 12./JG 27. 10. and 11. *Staffeln* were created from scratch, but also contained a considerable number of ex-III. *Gruppe* personnel. Command of IV./JG 27 was entrusted to Hauptmann Rudolf 'Rudi' Sinner who, for the past year, had been *Kapitän* of 6. *Staffel*.

The following weeks saw IV. *Gruppe* busy working up at Kalamaki, and suffering several casualties in the process, while III./JG 27 retired to Lecce to make good its numbers after its involvement in the creation of the former unit. A new 8. *Staffel* was set up in the first week of June. It was headed by Oberleutnant Wolf Ettel, who had been awarded the Knight's Cross only days earlier for his 120 eastern front victories with 4./JG 3.

With sunshades over their cockpits, a pair of G-6/trops of the newly activated IV./JG 27 bake in the noonday sun on the bare expanse of Tanagra airfield to the north-west of Athens in July 1943. Presumably the two aircraft of the *Alarmrotte*, ready to scramble at a moment's notice, both *Gustavs* ('Yellow 7' and 'Yellow 15') carry IV. *Gruppe's* unique double-horizontal-bar marking on the aft fuselage

Towards the end of June III. *Gruppe* moved back to Argos in Greece, with a *Schwarm* from Leutnant Emil Clade's 7. *Staffel* being detached to Máleme, on the island of Crete. Hardly had it resumed patrolling the Aegean approaches, however, when the Allied invasion of Sicily on 10 July caused the *Staffel* to be recalled post-haste to Brindisi, in Italy.

With their Bf 109s fitted with long-range tanks, the pilots flew their first ground-support missions over eastern Sicily on 15 July. Here, Wolf Ettel claimed his 121st kill (a Spitfire). He added another in the same area early the following morning, plus a pair of B-24s over southern Italy shortly after midday. But III./JG 27 had lost six of its own *Gustavs* during these two days. And worse was to come 24 hours later.

On 17 July five of the *Gruppe's* fighters were downed by flak while attacking British troops south of Catania. Four pilots perished, including the *Kapitän* of 8. *Staffel*, whose G-6 took a direct hit. Oberleutnant Wolf Ettel would be honoured with posthumous Oak Leaves on 31 August.

By that time III./JG 27 had long since been withdrawn from Brindisi. Following the now usual practice of passing its few remaining serviceable machines to other *Jagdgruppen* in the area (probably I./JG 53 and IV./JG 3), the unit entrained for Austria, and another round of re-equipment. This left the untried IV. *Gruppe* as sole guardians of the eastern Mediterranean and Aegean, which was the situation as *Kommodore* Major Gustav Rödel found it when he led the *Geschwaderstab* into Kalamaki.

IV./JG 27 had already opened its scoring by then, bringing down two out of a force of 23 unescorted B-24s which had bombed 12. *Staffel's* base at Máleme (killing one unfortunate armourer) on 9 July.

But it was a much bigger, and much better known, raid by another force of unescorted B-24s which provided IV. *Gruppe* with its next successes. In the early morning of 1 August a total of 178 Liberators had taken off from their desert bases around Benghazi for the 200-mile (3200-km) round-trip to the Ploesti oil refineries in Rumania. They were tracked by Luftwaffe radar for much of the way, and although IV./JG 27 did not participate in the historic air battles close to the target area, ten of its *Gustavs,* led by Oberleutnant Alfred Burk, *Kapitän* of 11 *Staffel*, were vectored out late in the afternoon to await a group of surviving B-24s reported to be clearing the Albanian coast prior to the final leg of their flight back across the Mediterranean to Libya.

An eastern front *Experte* with 120 victories to his credit, Oberleutnant Wolf Ettel, brought in as *Staffelkapitän* of the re-formed 8./JG 27, succumbed to ground fire while carrying out a low-level attack on British positions south of Catania in Sicily on 17 July

Kommodore Major Gustav Rödel makes the acquaintance of his new IV. *Gruppe* at Kalamaki in August as he accepts a cup of something refreshing. Playing mother is Unteroffizier Rudolf Philipp. Seated beneath the wing of the G-6 'gunship' are, from left to right, Oberleutnant Ernst-Georg Altnorthoff, Major Rödel, Oberleutnant Alfred Burk (StaKa 11./JG 27) and Feldwebel Ernst Hackl. These four IV. *Gruppe* pilots had each been credited with one of the five Ploesti B-24s brought down on 1 August (the fifth having been claimed by Leutnant Hans Flor)

The Bf 109s, almost at the limit of their endurance, intercepted the wave-hugging bombers west of the island of Cephalonia and claimed five of their number before shortage of fuel forced them to break off. One 10. *Staffel* pilot was brought down by the return fire as the B-24s fought their way southwards.

Little of import occurred in the weeks that followed until the unconditional surrender of Italy on 8 September 1943 suddenly threw a whole new complexion on operations in the Mediterranean.

The Italian collapse affected JG 27 in a number of ways. On a personal level it had already cost IV. *Gruppe* its first *Kommandeur*. Scapegoated for an 'unwarranted exchange of fire' with a neighbouring Italian army unit prior to the formal surrender, Hauptmann Rudolf Sinner was 'promoted sideways' to the command of IV./JG 54 on the eastern front in mid-September. His place was taken by acting *Kommandeur* Oberleutnant Dietrich Boesler.

Italy's defection from the Axis camp had also blown the Aegean wide open, for most of the islands in the region were garrisoned by Italian troops. Although German forces quickly occupied the 12 islands of the Dodecanese at the entrance to the Aegean, they were thinly spread at first, and unable to prevent the British from mounting landings on three of the main islands. Within two days Spitfires had flown in and were using the airstrips on Kós.

This threat to Greece and the Balkans (which had always been Churchill's preferred route into southern Europe) could not be ignored. III./JG 27 was rushed back down from Vienna to Argos, on the Peleponnese, and quickly sent detachments further south and eastwards to Crete and Rhodes. With IV. *Gruppe* likewise dispersed about the southern Aegean, the units' main activities in the weeks ahead would be focused on supporting the German re-conquest of those islands in the Dodecanese held by the British.

IV./JG 27 had already claimed its first five Spitfires off Kós on 18 and 19 September, prior to III. *Gruppe*'s arrival – but only at a cost of two of

A *Schwarm* of 7. *Staffel* Gustavs provide close escort for an He 111 VIP transport over the Aegean late in 1943. Flying the aircraft nearest the camera is *Schwarmführer* and *Staffelkapitän* of 7./JG 27, Leutnant Emil Clade. Yet oddly it is the second fighter in shot, 'White 9', which has the all-white vertical tail surfaces usually associated with a *Staffelkapitän's* machine (see colour profile 25).
Note that all three fighters are now wearing a standard III. *Gruppe* vertical bar marking. In addition, 'White 9' and 'White 7' both display the *Gruppe* badge on the cowling and 7. *Staffel's* new emblem beneath the cockpit . . .

. . . as does 'White 8', a G-6/trop 'gunboat' that came to grief at Máleme, on Crete, on 1 December. The *Staffel* emblem, depicting William Tell's apple in a gunsight, was chosen by competition, with the prize for the winning design being a special eight-day leave pass!

its own pilots reported missing. III./JG 27 destroyed seven Spitfires without loss in the same area on its first two days back in action, and would continue to exact a steady toll of Allied aircraft – over 100 in all – during this, its final period of Mediterranean service.

The *Gruppe's* most successful day was 8 October, which saw it bring down eight enemy machines of various types, including a highly suspect 'Manchester(!)' – more likely a B-25 – over southern Greece. And on seven separate sorties over the eastern Aegean during the first half of November its pilots were credited with an unbroken string of no fewer than 15 Beaufighters. After the forcible evacuation of the Spitfires from Kós, the twin-engined Beaufighter was the only British 'fighter' with sufficient range to reach the Dodecanese from RAF bases in Cyprus or Egypt. Once arrived, however, the bulky 'Beau' was at a distinct disadvantage if unlucky enough to be intercepted by III./JG 27's *Gustavs.*

During December, with the Dodecanese retaken, the *Gruppe's* opponents were mainly US 'heavies' over Greece. Four were shot down during a raid on Kalamaki (occupied by 9. *Staffel*) on 6 December, and another five while attacking Eleusis a fortnight later. On each occasion 7. *Staffel* suffered one pilot killed.

Major Rödel had also claimed a Beaufighter and a pair of 'heavies' since the *Geschwaderstab's* arrival in Greece. These, together with another two kills, took the *Kommodore's* total to 83. The only other pilot of the *Stab* to be credited with a victory over the eastern Mediterranean was Rödel's Adjutant, Oberleutnant Jost Schlang, who had sent a B-17 down west of Corinth on 10 October.

But it was IV. *Gruppe* who would score the most spectacular successes, and sustain the heaviest losses, as JG 27's long association with the Mediterranean theatre drew slowly but surely towards its close. Many of these final successes – nearly half, in fact – would be the work of just two pilots, both of whom were newcomers.

IV./JG 27's highest scorer was to be Feldwebel Heinrich Bartels, a ready-made *Experte* drafted in from JG 5 on the Arctic front. With 49 kills already to his credit, he was soon adding more. Here, he returns to Kalamaki, rocking his wings to indicate fresh victories. Note that IV. *Gruppe's Gustavs* now carry the wavy bar marking relinquished by III./JG 27

After acting *Kommandeur* Oberleutnant Dietrich Boesler had been killed in the action against B-17s near Corinth on 10 October, his official replacement nine days later was Hauptmann Joachim Kirschner, a 175-victory Oak Leaves wearer, who had latterly been serving on the eastern front as *Kapitän* of 5./JG 3.

Also recently arrived from Russia, and now assigned to 11. *Staffel*, was Feldwebel Heinrich Bartels. Most of Bartel's 49 victories to date had been scored with 8./JG 5 in the far north, where he had been awarded the Knight's Cross. The sudden change in climate from arctic to sub-tropical had little effect on his shooting ability, however, as he had quickly demonstrated by downing a brace of Bostons off Kós on 1 October.

Between them, it was these two *Experten* who were responsible for the lion's share of IV./JG 27's rapidly lengthening list of kills. They rarely returned from a sortie without multiple victories – three P-38s for Heinrich Bartels on 8 October, two Spitfires and a P-38 for Joachim Kirschner on 23 October, and another trio of P-38s, plus a Whitley(!), for Bartels 48 hours after that.

But, as always, it was the movement of armies on the ground, not individual successes in the air, which dictated the course of events. And by late October 1943 Allied forces were firmly established in Italy and gradually fighting their way northwards. This posed a whole new threat to the Balkan countries, which were now separated from Allied air bases in Italy by only the 120-mile (190-km) width of the Adriatic.

The consequent upsurge in activity at its back resulted in the last of JG 27's many major redispositions within the Mediterranean theatre. Leaving III. *Gruppe* to guard Greece and Crete, IV./JG 27 was ordered north to Podgorica, in Yugoslavia, on 28 October.

Three days later a clash over the Adriatic coast just below the Albanian border ended with three more P-38s for 11./JG 27 (three for Bartels) but cost the *Staffel* its *Kapitän*, Oberleutnant Alfred Burk. 11./JG 27 would be particularly unlucky, losing two more leaders before the year was out. But there was no stopping Heinrich Bartels. Not surprisingly, both he and *Gruppenkommandeur* Joachim Kirschner were heavily involved in the operations of 15 November, which proved to be the most successful day of IV./JG 27's entire two-year history.

On that date the *Gruppe* was credited with 15 victories without loss. All but one of the kills were P-38s, with Bartels' quartet taking his total to

70. With three of the P-38s and the single B-25 of the day, Kirschner's score now stood at 185. Within 48 hours each had added another three, mainly as the result of an engagement with a formation of B-25s and their P-38 escort on 17 November.

The ever increasing Allied air activity in the Balkans – the attacks on coastal shipping along the Adriatic, the support of Communist partisan forces in Yugoslavia, the Italian-based 'heavies' flying high overhead to targets further afield – meant that IV./JG 27 was soon stretched to the limit, both operationally and geographically. Having transferred to Skopje early in December, the *Gruppe* would also deploy *Staffeln* and *Schwärme* to some half-dozen other fields, ranging from Mostar, in Yugoslavia, to the north, down to Devoli, in southern Albania.

The weight of Allied numbers also led, inevitably, to a growing list of casualties. Although a pair of P-40s and a Spitfire were shot down on 16 December, three of the *Gruppe's* own pilots failed to return. Worse was to come the following day. In two separate engagements with Spitfires five pilots were lost without being able to claim a single victory.

Three had been caught over the Albanian coast, while the other two, bounced out of the sun to the south of Mostar, were the *Gruppenkommandeur* and his wingman. Unlike the latter, Hauptmann Joachim Kirschner managed to bale out of his damaged machine. But although air searches were mounted almost immediately, no trace of Kirschner could be found. It was later reported that the Luftwaffe's 20th highest-scoring fighter pilot had been captured and executed by partisans of the 29th Communist Brigade.

Joachim Kirschner's replacement was the experienced, but relatively low-scoring, Hauptmann Otto Meyer who, for the past five months, had been *Staffelkapitän* of 4./JG 27. But the *Gruppe* which Meyer inherited was in a sorry state. On the last day of the year it mustered exactly a dozen serviceable *Gustavs*.

Credited with four of the fourteen P-38s claimed by IV. *Gruppe* on 15 November (one US source states that only two Lightnings were lost that day!), Bartels' score has risen to 70. His all-white rudder displays this latest total in seven neat rows of ten, each below a representation of the Knight's Cross won earlier while with JG 5. The actual award is also visible as Bartels (left) chats to fellow pilots

Gruppenkommandeur Hauptmann Joachim Kirschner had come to IV./JG 27 with even more eastern front victories to his credit. Pictured here in Russia, Kirschner added 13 kills while at the head of IV. *Gruppe*, taking his overall total to 188, before being shot down over Yugoslavia on 17 December 1943

Assuming command of III./JG 27 as a Hauptmann (as seen here) in October 1942, Major Ernst Düllberg's III. *Gruppe* was the last unit of *Jagdgeschwader* 27 to leave the Mediterranean theatre. Düllberg ended the war as *Kommodore* of JG 76. Some 37 of his 50 victories had been scored while serving with JG 27

Although this total was more than doubled during the opening weeks of 1944, IV./JG 27's involvement in the Balkans was coming to an end. The *Gruppe's* final action, on 24 January, was in defence of its own Skopje base, which was the target for a force of B-24s heavily escorted by P-38s. The *Gruppe* claimed two of the fighters, plus three bombers. One of the B-24s provided *Kommandeur* Otto Meyer with his 12th kill of the war.

Early in February IV./JG 27 moved eastwards to Nish, closer to Yugoslavia's border with Bulgaria. Here it would remain in relative inactivity for the best part of six weeks, before being ordered to withdraw to Graz, in Austria.

This left just Major Ernst Düllberg's III. *Gruppe* patrolling and protecting southern Greece and the Aegean. But the progress of the war on the other fronts meant that its days in the eastern Mediterranean were now also numbered. And after one last significant success on 9 February, which saw the unit's pilots credited with seven Beaufighters around Samos without loss to themselves, III./JG 27 too received orders the following month to retire to Austria.

This was not quite the end, however, for Düllberg had been instructed to leave behind his 7. *Staffel*. Commanded by Leutnant Hans-Gunnar Culemann and strengthened to more than double its official establishment, this '*Staffel*' would remain in Greece and Crete for another two months. It alone was thus responsible for JG 27's final 25+ Mediterranean victories. On 6 March, for example, members of the *Staffel* were credited with six B-26s to the north-west of Crete.

But it was a particular irony that the very last kills of all should be machines of their erstwhile Axis partner, for the formation of tri-motored transports which 7./JG 27 caught over the Straits of Otranto on the afternoon of 14 May 1944 were SM.84s of the Italian Co-Belligerent Air Force operating on the side of the Allies. Six of their number were sent down into the sea north-east of Brindisi in the space of just ten minutes.

And the sting in the tail is that it was return fire from these self-same ex-partners which resulted in the loss of Unteroffizier Gerhard Siegling, the last of more than 150 pilots of JG 27 reported killed or missing in the Mediterranean theatre since I. *Gruppe's* arrival at Ain-el-Gazala just over three years earlier.

THE FINAL BATTLES

The story of JG 27's final months is briefly, if perhaps a little unfairly, told. Briefly, because once the *Geschwader* had withdrawn from the Mediterranean back into the Reich, it became involved in a repetitive war of attrition against an impersonal foe. Unfairly perhaps because these operations, fought against the established might of the US daylight bombing offensive, witnessed some of the fiercest confrontations, and resulted in by far the heaviest losses, of any period in the unit's history.

But before reviewing the massed air battles against the combined, and ever growing, weight of the US Eighth and Fifteenth Air Forces, what of I./JG 27,which had been evacuated from Arco Philaenorum, in Libya, early in November 1942 and, unlike the rest of the *Geschwader*, had then left the Mediterranean theatre altogether?

Commanded since the time of the move by Hauptmann Heinrich Setz – brought in from JG 77, where his 135 victories had already earned him the Oak Leaves – I. *Gruppe* had staged via Italy and Germany to Evreux, in northern France. Here, it re-equipped with G-4s and began working up with a large intake of young pilots fresh from training school. Thus, with new aircraft, a high proportion of new pilots, and a new *Kommandeur*, the *Gruppe* bore little relationship to the I./JG 27 of its desert heydays. And the Channel front was now also very different to that of the Battle of Britain period three years earlier. It was certainly no respecter of reputations.

On one of its earliest operations, I. *Gruppe* was scrambled from Bernay on 13 March 1943 to intercept a large formation of Spitfires 'ramrodding' into northern France. In the subsequent engagement near Amiens, Heinrich Setz managed to claim three of the intruders, after which he himself disappeared. The *Kommandeur's* body was later discovered in the wreckage of his *Gustav* some miles east of Le Tréport, the victim, it is believed, of a mid-air collision with one of the enemy.

It is a telling indication of I./JG 27's changing fortunes that Hauptmann Setz had been only the fourth *Kommandeur* since the

Portrayed as an Oberleutnant, and seen wearing the Oak Leaves won in June 1942 when *Staffelkapitän* of 4./JG 77 in Russia, Hauptmann Heinrich Setz, *Kommandeur* of I. *Gruppe*, was killed over the French Channel coast on 13 March 1943 after claiming a trio of Canadian Spitfires

While the bulk of I./JG 27 was based at Bernay and Poix, in France, during the spring and early summer of 1943, the G-4 'gunboats' of Oberleutnant Josef Jansen's 2. *Staffel* were detached to Leeuwarden, in the Netherlands. Note the retention of I. *Gruppe's* famous *Afrika* badge

103

Transferred in from JG 2 to replace the fallen Heinrich Setz, Knight's Cross-holder Hauptmann Erich Hohagen claimed just two victories (a Ventura and a Mitchell) over the Channel as *Kommandeur* of I. *Gruppe* before being wounded on 1 June. After recovering, Hohagen – pictured here (left) with Oberleutnant Fritz Dettmann – would return to operations, only to be wounded again, more seriously, on the western front in the autumn of 1944. By the end of the war he was flying the Me 262 with Adolf Galland's JV 44

Gruppe's formation in 1939. In the remaining two years of its existence there would be no fewer than 17!

In fact, Setz was but one of 14 fatalities suffered by I./JG 27, with nearly as many again wounded, during the *Gruppe's* four-month tour of duty in defence of north-west Europe. Throughout this time it operated primarily under the control of JG 2, but was also attached briefly to JG 26 as and when circumstances dictated. In addition, 2. *Staffel* spent several weeks on detachment to Leeuwarden, in the Netherlands, alongside II./JG 1.

Despite all its difficulties, I./JG 27 would be credited with over 40 victories, ranging from low-level Venturas to high-flying B-17s. Its most successful action took place on 18 May when the *Gruppe* claimed seven Typhoons flying a ramrod to Cayeux (No 3 Sqn RAF admitted to the loss of five of their machines, including one to ground-fire). And three days later the Dutch-based 2. *Staffel* reportedly shot down five B-17s engaged on a raid against Emden.

Then, in June, the bulk of the *Gruppe* was suddenly transferred to Marignane, in southern France, where it was to spend several uneventful weeks, before being recalled to the homeland at the end of July 1943.

After a short stop-over at Münster, during which time it claimed seven B-17s in the Bonn area on 12 August, I./JG 27 took up residence at Fels am

This pair of brand-new G-6 'gunboats' of I./JG 27 were photographed after the *Gruppe's* transfer to Fels am Wagram, in Austria, in August 1943, and their subsequent incorporation into the Defence of the Reich organisation. They now wore JG 27's sage-green aft fuselage bands . . .

... seen here more clearly on 1. *Staffel's* 'White 4', undergoing maintenance on the flightline at Fels

For a brief period while at Fels 3./JG 27 paid homage to their past by invoking the name of the unit's most illustrious *Staffelkapitän*, the late Hans-Joachim Marseille. Here, Oberleutnant Fritz Dettmann points to their own special version of the *Gruppe* badge, with its wide border bearing the inscription *STAFFEL MARSEILLE*

Wagram, in Austria, later that same month. This one-time training field to the west of Vienna would be the unit's principal base for the next ten months. Its role was now the defence of south-east Europe from the US heavy bombers, soon to be constituted as the Fifteenth Air Force, flying up across the Alps, or over the Danubian plain, from the Mediterranean and Italy.

I./JG 27's young pilots rose to the challenge. In the course of some 20 major engagements they were credited with close on 190 American aircraft destroyed. The vast majority of their victims were heavy bombers, including well over 100 B-24s and 60+ B-17s.

On two occasions, on 2 November 1943 and 23 February 1944, when the Fifteenth Air Force attacked Austrian aircraft and component factories at Wiener Neustadt and Steyr respectively, they claimed no fewer than 16

Two stills from a German newsreel, shown in cinemas in March 1944, capturing the drama of an *Alarmstart* (emergency scramble) from a snow-covered Fels in the winter of 1943/44

B-24s in a single action (during the Steyr raid in the space of just 20 minutes!). And their top-scoring day against the Fifteenth's B-17s was on 25 February 1944 when they accounted for 13 Fortresses over the Alps to the north of Klagenfurt.

But these victories were gained at a price. The *Gruppe* lost some 20 pilots killed or missing in action, plus many more wounded. These figures included four *Kommandeure*, two wounded and two killed. The two fatalities were both old Africa hands. Hauptmann Hans Remmer died when he attempted to bale out at too low an altitude after claiming his 27th, and final, victory, a B-24 west of Graz on 2 April. He would be awarded a posthumous Knight's Cross two months later.

Major Karl-Wolfgang Redlich was already wearing the Knight's Cross, won in Africa as *Kapitän* of 1. *Staffel*, when he was recalled from a staff

1./JG 27's *Staffelkapitän*, Hauptmann Hans Remmer, was serving as acting *Kommandeur* of I. *Gruppe* when he was killed in action against Fifteenth Air Force B-24s attacking Steyr, in Austria, on 2 April 1944. He would be honoured with a posthumous Knight's Cross on 30 June . . .

. . . by which time I./JG 27 had lost three more *Kommandeure*, two wounded and one killed. The first to be wounded was old desert hand Major Ludwig 'Ziskus' Franzisket, who baled out of his 'Black Double Chevron' – possibly the green-banded, white-ruddered *Gustav* he is pictured flying here – near Frankfurt on 12 May 1944. At year's end Franzisket would return as *Kommodore* to lead JG 27 during the final months of the war

position to take over the *Gruppe* after the wounding of Hauptmann Ernst Börngen on 19 May. 'Papa' Redlich lasted just ten days. He too was killed after shooting down a B-24 – his one and only heavy bomber out of a total score of 43 – near St Pölten on 29 May. Major Redlich would be the last casualty of I./JG 27's final confrontation with the Fifteenth Air Force over the south-eastern corner of Hitler's *Festung Europa*, for eight days later Allied troops stormed ashore in Normandy. Suddenly it was the north-western ramparts of the Führer's 'fortress' which were facing the greater peril.

I./JG 27's arrival at Fels am Wagram in August 1943 had coincided with the return of Hauptmann Werner Schroer's II. *Gruppe* from Italy. It too would now form part of the aerial defence of the Reich, but not based in Austria. Stationed instead in the Rhineland area – primarily at Wiesbaden-Erbenheim, but with temporary deployments as far removed as Eelde and Twente, in Holland, St Dizier, in France, as well as other fields in both north and south Germany – II./JG 27's main adversary in the months ahead was to be the 'Mighty Eighth'.

Like I./JG 27 in Austria, its victims would be exclusively American, and, for the most part, heavy bombers. But reflecting the composition of the Eighth Air Force, the preponderance of the 'heavies' the *Gruppe* destroyed would be B-17s – nearly 90 in all. Another difference between I. and II. *Gruppen* was that the latter were engaging the intruders from the north on a more frequent basis, and thus achieved their 120+ victories by a process of steady attrition, rather than in a series of spectacular single actions. I./JG 27's highest score on any one day during this period was the nine 'heavies', and single P-47, claimed over the Netherlands on 11 January 1944.

Exactly one week after Franzisket took to his parachute, his successor, Hauptmann Ernst Börngen, was seriously wounded when he too was forced to bale out after ramming a B-24 near Helmstedt. Börngen had claimed two Liberators during the engagement which saw the end of his combat career (begun with a pair of Spitfires on 18 August 1940), for doctors were unable to save his right arm. He would be awarded the Knight's Cross on 3 August

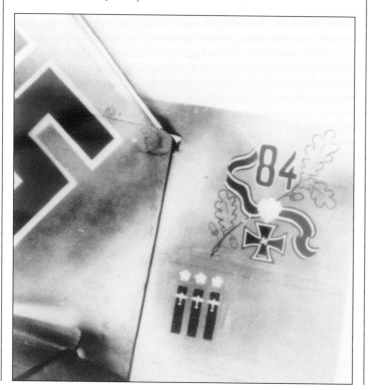

It was also a brace of B-24s, brought down near Bari, in Italy, on 16 July 1943, which had won Hauptmann Werner Schroer, *Gruppenkommandeur* of II./JG 27, the Oak Leaves. The award is recorded here on the otherwise white rudder of his *Gustav*, together with three Eighth Air Force B-17s added after the *Gruppe's* arrival at Wiesbaden-Erbenheim for Reich's Defence duties

Two pilots would add double figures to their existing totals during this period. The *Kommandeur* himself, recently awarded the Oak Leaves for 84 kills and promoted to major in the interim, took his tally to one short of a century – the 99th was a P-38 downed over Magdeburg on 3 March 1944. Ten days later he would be appointed *Kommandeur* of III./JG 54. Major Werner Schroer ended the war as *Kommodore* of JG 3 'Udet', wearing the Swords and with a final score of 114.

One of Schroer's *Staffelkapitäne*, Oberleutnant Willie Kientsch of 6./JG 27, added a round dozen to his personal score. On 22 November he was awarded the Knight's Cross for his 43 victories. It was the first such decoration for the *Geschwader* in almost a year. The previous one had been presented to 5. *Staffel's* Leutnant Karl-Heinz Bendert – for 42 kills – on 30 December 1942 while II./JG 27 was 'resting' in Germany after its withdrawal from North Africa.

The *Gruppe's* successes were dearly bought, however. By the end of May 1944 over 50 pilots had been reported killed or missing in action, with another 30 wounded – twice the unit's official complement! Among the dead were four *Staffelkapitäne*. One, 5./JG 27's Oberleutnant Herbert Schramm, was a Knight's Cross holder from JG 53. Shot down by P-47s over Belgium on 1 December 1943, Schramm's final total of 42 – including a trio of B-17s claimed while serving with JG 27 – would be recognised by posthumous Oak Leaves early in 1945.

6./JG 27's Oberleutnant Willie Kientsch would be similarly honoured. The recent Knight's Cross winner was killed during a low-level dogfight over the hills south of Koblenz on 29 January 1944. His final score of 53, which resulted in posthumous Oak Leaves on 20 July, included 20 heavy bombers.

Badly understrength, II./JG 27 was withdrawn from central Germany in the first week of June 1944. It were ordered to Fels am Wagram (vacated by I. *Gruppe* only hours earlier) to rest and re-equip with new machines.

During the final weeks of its campaign against the Fifteenth Air Force in the south-east, I./JG 27 had been joined by the *Geschwaderstab* and IV. *Gruppe* up from the Balkans, and by III. *Gruppe* returning from southern Greece and the Aegean.

Oberstleutnant Gustav Rödel's *Stab* had flown in to Fels am Wagram at the end of February 1944. Still 'leading from the front', the *Kommodore* would be responsible for 11 of the 25 kills credited to the *Stab* during its time in the Vienna area (on 13 May it had moved from Fels to Wien-Seyring, close to the Austrian capital).

Major Ernst Düllberg's III./JG 27 arrived at Wien-Seyring early in March, but its promised period of rest and recuperation was short-lived. On 19 March raids on a number of Austrian airfields saw the unit thrown back into the thick of the fighting. Its pilots claimed 13 B-24s from a force attacking Graz for the loss of two of their own. On 2 April nine more B-24s were downed over southern Styria at the cost of one missing.

And so it had gone on. After brief deployment to bases in Hungary and Yugoslavia in mid-April, III. *Gruppe* returned to Wien-Götzendorf early in May. From this field to the south-east of Vienna, the unit found itself engaged not only against the Fifteenth Air Force, but also the Eighth Air Force flying down from the north. This resulted in the *Gruppe* playing the

With his score standing at 99, the now Major Werner Schroer was appointed *Gruppenkommandeur* of III./JG 54 on 13 March 1944

leading role in the last three major successes against US 'heavies' ever to be achieved by the *Geschwader*.

On 12 May 1944 the Eighth Air Force targeted Germany's oil industry for the first time. Intercepting one of the bomber streams near Frankfurt, III./JG 27 claimed 13 B-17s for the loss of three pilots. On the same date the *Stab* was credited with six B-17s, I. *Gruppe* with seven (plus two P-51s) and II. *Gruppe* with five – thirty-one heavy bombers in all!

Twelve days later it was the turn of the Fifteenth Air Force to suffer at the hands of III./JG 27, losing 16 B-24s during yet more raids on Luftwaffe airfields in Austria. In addition, the *Stab* claimed another three, I. *Gruppe* a further twelve and IV. *Gruppe* three B-24s and a brace of B-17s – a total of thirty-six bombers!

By contrast, the 16 B-17s claimed by JG 27 (13 by III. *Gruppe*) on 28 May, when the Eighth Air Force again mounted a major effort against the Reich's oil targets, seem almost an anti-climax.

Although some of the above victories were officially listed as *Herausschüsse* (literally 'shootings-out' – i.e. damaging a bomber to such an extent that it was forced to drop out of its combat box, and thus become a prime target for 'final destruction'), never again would the *Geschwader* enjoy such success. During the final 11 months of the war, in fact, rarely would any one day's total of kills reach double figures.

By the end of May III./JG 27's operations in defence of the Reich had added exactly 90 heavy bombers (plus three fighters) to the *Gruppe's* collective scoreboard. *Kommandeur* Ernst Düllberg had contributed just four to that figure. The most successful pilot of this period was the veteran Leutnant Dr Peter Werfft, now *Kapitän* of 9. *Staffel*, whose score had risen from 12 to 22 before he was wounded on 19 May.

Also arriving back in Austria in March, Hauptmann Otto Meyer's IV./JG 27 had spent most of its time since based at Steinamanger and Vat, in Hungary. Unlike I. and III. *Gruppen*, almost exactly half of its 51 victories were made up of fighters, including a trio of Spitfires caught over Croatia on 23 April. These three RAF machines, plus another nine US fighters, ensured that Feldwebel Heinrich Bartels retained his position as the *Gruppe's* highest scorer with 85. *Kommandeur* Otto Meyer's six kills during this period included five 'heavies'. But mention should also be made of the two P-51s claimed by Leutnant Ernst-Wilhelm Reinert, the *Kapitän* of 12. *Staffel*. Recently arrived from JG 77 with a total of 166, Reinert was already wearing the Oak Leaves.

It is reported that Reinert had been recommended for the Swords, but not only was this recommendation turned down, it also led to his transfer to JG 27. It appears that the *Kommodore* of JG 77 did not relish having a subordinate whose successes challenged, and at times surpassed, his own high scores and awards. This *Kommodore*, incidentally, was the same Johannes Steinhoff who had likewise dumped a certain unruly young Oberfähnrich on to JG 27 four years earlier!

The make-up of IV. *Gruppe* – the majority of its pilots young and fairly inexperienced, but stiffened by a core of veteran NCOs and officers, and with one or two high-scoring, highly-decorated individuals at its head – mirrored the situation of JG 27 as a whole when the invasion of Normandy on 6 June 1944 saw the bulk of the *Geschwader* transferred post-haste from Austria and the south-east up into northern France.

Not unnaturally, it would be the younger, less experienced pilots, and their even more sketchily trained replacements, whose names would dominate the lengthening casualty lists as Oberstleutnant Rödel's *Stab*, together with I., III. and IV. *Gruppen*, faced the now massive weight of Anglo-American air power supporting the invasion forces.

Yet despite sustaining a swingeing 130+ combat casualties (some two-thirds of whom were killed or reported missing) during the defence of Normandy and subsequent retreat through Belgium, JG 27's losses were still outweighed – just – by their successes. Such numerical comparisons lose a lot of their meaning, however, when the two sides' reserves are added to the equation. The Allies could quickly make good their combat losses. The Luftwaffe, on the other hand, while perhaps still able to replace most of their rank and file casualties, could ill afford the steady drain of experienced fighter leaders.

In Normandy the situation soon became so critical that *Reichsmarschall* Göring was forced to introduce a scale, based on the number of aircraft involved, limiting the sorties flown by his fighter commanders. *Staffelkapitäne* could only take to the air when leading a formation of at least six machines, *Gruppenkommandeure* fifteen, and *Geschwaderkommodoren* 45!

It was this rule which, in all probability, cost Gustav Rödel his century. The *Kommodore* and his *Stab* arrived at Champfleury, some 60 miles (95 km) east south-east of Paris late on D-Day itself. In the month that followed it claimed a dozen kills, all US fighters. Oberstleutnant Rödel was credited with four of them, the last, a P-38, going down on 5 July. It

Pictured (left) while serving with JG 77 in Tunisia, Leutnant Ernst-Wilhelm Reinert became *Staffelkapitän* of 12./JG 27 on 13 May 1944 and then went on to replace Hanns-Heinz Dudeck as *Kommandeur* of IV. *Gruppe* on 2 January 1945 after the latter failed to return from Operation *Bodenplatte*. Of interest here is the *Kübelwagen* (German jeep) against which Reinert is leaning. It would seem that fighters were not the only items that I./JG 27 bequeathed to JG 77 when it left Africa. The *Gruppe* must have handed over some of its vehicles too, for *OTTO* – decorated with a variety of native fauna – was once the favourite desert runabout of Hans-Joachim Marseille

Oberst Gustav Rödel's 98th, and final, kill was a P-38 downed over the Normandy front on 5 July 1944. It was also the last of the 82 victories credited to the *Geschwaderstab* during the course of the war, of which Rödel alone had been responsible for no fewer than 28. On 29 December Oberst Rödel was appointed to the staff of 2. *Jagd-Division*, which he then commanded from February to April 1945

was Gustav Rödel's 98th, and final, victory, for on that date Göring's restricting order came into force – and rarely thereafter did the *Geschwader* manage to put 45 fighters into the air at any one time.

Rödel's three *Gruppen* had joined him in France by D+1. IV./JG 27 took up quarters at Champfleury alongside the *Stab,* while I. and III./JG 27 were based nearby at Vertus and Connantre respectively. After months of battling US 'heavies' in the south, the *Gruppen's* pilots were suddenly fighting a very different kind of war, mainly at low-level and against overwhelming numbers of Allied fighters and fighter-bombers.

Some made the transition more easily than others. On 12 June (D+6) Hauptmann Otto Meyer's IV. *Gruppe* claimed nine P-47s west of Evreux – three for the *Kommandeur* himself – at a cost of one pilot killed and five wounded. Forty-eight hours later it was credited with another eight P-47s, plus a pair of B-17s, without loss. The latter occasion provided the seemingly unstoppable Heinrich Bartels with the first four of his Normandy victories. On the other side of the coin, IV./JG 27 was the only *Gruppe* to lose its *Kommandeur* over the invasion beachhead when Hauptmann Otto Meyer – his final score standing at 21 – was reported missing in the Caen area on 12 July.

Within a fortnight of Meyer's loss the *Gruppe,* headed now by Hauptmann Hanns-Heinz Dudeck, had been reduced to just nine service-able *Gustavs.* The survivors fought on, but were able to claim only three more victories before being withdrawn to Germany in mid-August.

Major Ernst Düllberg's III./JG 27 came a close second in the numbers of Allied aircraft destroyed over Normandy, claiming just seven fewer than IV. *Gruppe's* total of 58. But it paid an even heavier price – and not only in personnel. On 24 June Allied fighter-bombers struck at Connantre, destroying a dozen of the *Gruppe's* G-6s and damaging others. Although the unit was able to bring down six US fighters three days later, and another ten in the fortnight that followed, it suffered 20 casualties during the same period. By the middle of July the remaining pilots had been ordered back to Germany, where they would spend the next four weeks trying to prepare a whole new intake of young and under-trained officer cadets and NCOs for the battles ahead.

III./JG 27 returned to France on 15 August, just as I. *Gruppe* was with-drawing from the invasion front. Since arriving at Vertus, I./JG 27 had occupied a number of bases along the southern and western flanks of the Allied bridgehead – even spending the best part of a week at Vannes, on the Atlantic coast. It was the only *Gruppe* of the three whose casualties in the Normandy campaign exceeded its claims, hence its departure in mid-August for Hoya, south-west of Bremen, for urgently needed rest and refit.

III. *Gruppe* had marked its arrival back in France – at a heavily-camouflaged forward landing strip north of Paris, to be exact – by shooting down 17 Allied fighters in the first four days. Six had been Typhoons claimed on 17 August (No 183 Sqn's records indicate four machines lost in the Falaise region on that date). One of the Typhoons, plus a P-51 24 hours later, took *Kommandeur* Ernst Düllberg's total to 37, and won him the Knight's Cross.

But the *Gruppe's* new and inexperienced young NCO pilots were being hit hard. Ten had already become casualties, and further losses would be sustained before III./JG 27 withdrew to St Trond, in Belgium, on 28 August, and thence to Köln (Cologne)-Wahn eight days later. While at Cologne the *Gruppe* operated briefly against the airborne landings around Arnhem, claiming a P-51 over Nijmegen on 19 September, but losing one of its own in return.

On the last day of September Major Ernst Düllberg was appointed *Kommodore* of JG 76, a recently established homeland defence unit. III./JG 27 would continue to operate over the western front during the first half of October, but achieved only three victories for the loss of seven more of its NCOs. By mid-month the unit had retired to Grossenhain, north-west of Dresden, where it would exchange its remaining G-6s and G-14s (the latter first taken on charge only two months earlier) for brand new Bf 109K-4s.

While Rödel's three *Gruppen* had been suffering the blood-letting of the Normandy campaign and its aftermath, Hauptmann Fritz Keller's II./JG 27 had taken over its duties as defenders of the Reich's south-easternmost borders. Arriving at Fels am Wagram on 7 June, the precise nature of the *Gruppe's* new role became apparent with the delivery of some 60 Bf 109G-6/AS fighters, a special high-altitude version of the standard Messerschmitt workhorse.

Thus equipped, II./JG 27 commenced operations on 2 July. The omens were not good, for the cost of knocking a single B-24 out of a formation attacking Budapest on this date was seven fighters lost, with two pilots killed and five wounded!

Although this disastrous kill-to-loss ratio would not be repeated, the *Gruppe's* performance over the next two months gave little cause for

II. *Gruppe's* conversion on to the high-altitude G-6/AS was not without incident, as this picture all too clearly shows. Oberfeldwebel Alfred Müller of 4./JG 27 poses somewhat sheepishly beside the spectacular remains of his *Gustav* during training at Fels am Wagram in June 1944. Müller already had eight victories to his credit, and he would double that number (his final total including five USAAF 'heavies') before being killed in action on 16 August

jubilation. By the end of August it had brought down 15 US 'heavies', and two dozen of their escorting fighters, over south-east Europe. But 30 of the unit's pilots had been killed or reported missing, and a further 15 wounded, in the process.

By this time the Normandy break-out was well underway. Allied troops were across the Seine and, with the invasion beachhead secured, the heavy bombers of the Eighth Air Force were once again focusing their attention on targets within the Reich. This in turn resulted in the transfer of II./JG 27 from Austria to Finsterwalde, some 60 miles (95 km) south south-east of Berlin. But the skies of central and western Germany – the *Gruppe* moved from Finsterwalde to Gütersloh on 17 September – were now more dangerous than ever before. During the month the *Gruppe* managed to claim 12 victories, including a high-flying Mosquito over Halberstadt (its first RAF victim for more than a year) and five P-47s in a dogfight close to the Dutch border. These successes had come at a high price, however. Of the 17 casualties suffered, twelve had been killed – six on 11 September alone, a day which had seen another major raid by the Eighth Air Force on Germany's synthetic oil plants and refineries.

It was during this period (the official date being 15 August) – when all four *Gruppen* were either transferring, resting or re-equipping – that JG 27 was re-organised on the four-*Staffel*-per-*Gruppe* basis being introduced throughout the *Jagdwaffe*. The somewhat complicated process of redesignation and assimilation of new strength is most simply illustrated by the following table:

During the less than three weeks it spent at Finsterwalde (29 August to 17 September) II./JG 27 claimed just four victories. In the same period it suffered nine pilots killed. But for those who remained the fight went on. Here, at the *Gruppe's* base to the south of Berlin, Generalleutnant Josef Schmid, GOC I. *Jagdkorps*, awards the Iron Cross to a youthful-looking – but unfortunately unidentified – pilot

I./JG 27	1. *Staffel*	- as before
	2. *Staffel*	- as before
	3. *Staffel*	- as before
	4. *Staffel*	- ex-14./JG 27*
II./JG 27	5. *Staffel*	- as before
	6. *Staffel*	- as before
	7. *Staffel*	- ex-4. *Staffel*
	8. *Staffel*	- new
III./JG 27	9. *Staffel*	- as before
	10. *Staffel*	- ex-13./JG 27*
	11. *Staffel*	- ex-8. *Staffel*
	12. *Staffel*	- ex-7.*Staffel*
IV./JG 27	13 *Staffel*	- ex-10. *Staffel*
	14. *Staffel*	- ex-12./JG 27*
	15. *Staffel*	- ex-11. *Staffel*
	16. *Staffel*	- ex-15./JG 27*

* First activated May – June 1944.

With each *Staffel* having an official establishment of 15 aircraft, plus reserves, this meant that every *Gruppe* now numbered over 60 fighters, III./JG 27 being fully re-equipped with the K-4, II./JG 27 continuing to operate its specialised high-altitude late model *Gustavs*, and I. and IV./JG 27 flying G-14s (but later also converting predominantly to K-4s).

The *Geschwader's* peak strength in the early autumn of 1944 of some 250 machines – the highest in its entire history – was, however, more a tribute to the tenacity and adaptability of Germany's aircraft manufacturers rather than evidence of a resurgence in JG 27's fortunes. Thanks to the Eighth and Fifteenth Air Forces' combined bombing campaigns against the oil industry, the *Jagdwaffe's* fuel situation was already critical, and beginning to border on the catastrophic. And the majority of its pilots were now either youngsters, even more inadequately trained than ever before, or veteran flyers from defunct multi-engined bomber and reconnaissance units with little or no experience of fighter combat.

The illusory nature of JG 27's greatly increased strength was quickly revealed. On 2 November the Eighth Air Force mounted yet another major raid on the Reich's synthetic oil installations. Operating for the first time as a complete Reichs-Defence *Geschwader*, all four *Gruppen* engaged the force of 600+ B-17s attacking Merseburg/Leuna, but were completely unable to penetrate the bombers' screen of escorting fighters. They did not destroy a single B-17, but *were* credited with six P-51s shot down.

These half-dozen Mustangs cost JG 27 a staggering 50 Bf 109s, with some 27 pilots being killed (11 from I. *Gruppe* and 10 from IV.) and 12 others wounded. Among III./JG 27's five fatalities was the *Kapitän* of 10. *Staffel*, Hauptmann Ernst-Ascan Gobert, an ex-bomber pilot who had won the Knight's Cross while serving with KG 53.

The losses of 2 November – the highest by far ever suffered in a single day by JG 27 – marked the beginning of the end for the *Geschwader*. By mid-December a further 39 pilots had been killed and 14 wounded, mostly over Germany's north-west border provinces – a total of almost 100 pilots lost in little more than six months. Included in that figure were two *Gruppenkommandeure*, killed in action against Allied fighters within 24 hours of each other, and three *Staffelkapitäne*.

During this period JG 27's claims numbered 43. They were not shared equally between the *Gruppen*, but ranged from III./JG 27's two P-51s to IV. *Gruppe's* 21 kills. Unusual among the latter were the eight Lancasters (three of them *Herausschüsse*), part of a force of 140 RAF 'heavies' attacking the Ruhr in daylight, which were credited to IV./JG 27 on 12 December.

Four days later Hitler launched his surprise counter-offensive in the Ardennes. Timed to coincide with a forecast period of bad weather which, it was hoped, would keep most of the Allies' UK-based air strength grounded, the first few days of the 'Battle of the Bulge' saw JG 27 facing 'only' those aircraft of the Anglo-American tactical forces operating from mainland Europe.

Even then it barely managed to hold its own. On 17 December IV. *Gruppe* destroyed seven USAAF fighters for the loss of six *Gustavs* (and one pilot). II. *Gruppe* was less fortunate, for its quartet of Thunderbolts cost the unit some eight machines, with three pilots killed and four wounded.

An improvement in the weather on 23 December, and consequent all-out air support for the embattled US ground troops, immediately made itself felt. In the last week of 1944 the *Geschwader* would lose a further 50 pilots either killed, missing or wounded. It was on 23 December that 7. *Staffel's* Unteroffizier Hermann Kässinger achieved his first success – the *Herausschuss* of a B-17 south of Trier. The 94th BG's *Darling Dot* (aka *Big Gas Bird*) would be the last of the nearly 550 'heavies' credited to JG 27 during the war.

On that same 23 December IV. *Gruppe* lost its most successful pilot. Moments after claiming his 99th kill (a P-47 just south of Bonn), Oberfeldwebel Heinrich Bartels was himself shot down. Already nominated for the Oak Leaves at the time of his death, Bartels' remains, still in the wreckage of his 'Yellow 13', would lay undiscovered for almost a quarter of a century.

Bartels' skills had been greatly respected by his fellow pilots in 15. *Staffel*. One individual remarked, 'To fly on Bartels' wing was almost as good as a life insurance!' And if someone of his experience could be brought down, what chance for the many teenaged replacements now forming an ever larger part of JG 27? Some of the latter were already giving cause for concern, as was apparent from an *Ultra* intercept of Oberst Gustav Rödel's report on his *Geschwader's* performance during the action of 23 December. When decrypted, this revealed that Rödel estimated some 20 per cent of his pilots had broken off their attacks (on a formation of B-17s) without good reason, had jettisoned their ventral fuel tanks and returned to base prematurely. He concluded by threatening to court-martial any who did so in future!

Oberst Rödel had little time to carry out his threat, even had it been proven necessary. On 29 December he was appointed to the staff of 2. *Jagd-Division*. It thus fell to Major Ludwig Franzisket – the same 'Ziskus' whose long service with the *Geschwader* dated back to the beginning of the war when he was a Leutnant with I./JG 1 – to oversee JG 27 during its final weeks.

All four *Gruppen* participated in Operation *Bodenplatte*, the New Year's Day attack by the Luftwaffe on Allied airfields in Belgium, Holland and France. Compared to other units taking part, the *Geschwader's* strike against its assigned objective, Brussels-Melsbroek, was undoubtedly a success, and its losses below average.

Taking off at sunrise on 1 January 1945 from its bases to the north and west of Osnabrück, JG 27's 70+ Bf 109s, accompanied by 15 Fw 190s of IV./JG 54, flew a low-level dog-leg course over Utrecht, in Holland, which would lead them down to Melsbroek from the north. Whether a deliberate ploy or not, this unexpected route of approach seems to have caught Melsbroek's defenders unawares. Two of the field's three resident Mitchell squadrons had taken off on a bombing mission before JG 27's arrival, but it is reported that some of the ground personnel were seen waving at the oncoming German fighters!

Each pilot had been ordered to carry out four separate strafing runs. Most succeeded in doing so, ignoring the 'late and fairly ineffective flak'. Sources differ as to the exact amount of damage caused during the 40-minute onslaught, but it appears that 34(PR) Wing was hit hard, losing eleven Wellingtons, five Mosquitos and three Spitfires destroyed, plus others damaged. In addition, four Mitchells, another two Spitfires, nine communications aircraft, a solitary Stirling and several visiting US machines were also totally wrecked, with yet more damaged. In the air, the attackers encountered, and shot down, two Spitfires and an Auster.

This carnage would cost JG 27 18 pilots killed, captured or wounded. At least 11 of the casualties were suffered during the approach and return flights, with a number falling victim to 'friendly' flak over German-held territory. One of the three PoWs was Hauptmann Hanns-Heinz Dudeck, *Kommandeur* of IV. *Gruppe*, who baled out after his G-10 was hit by anti-aircraft fire over Venray, in the Netherlands, while returning to IV./JG 27's base at Achmer.

Although the *Geschwader* had emerged from *Bodenplatte* with relatively light losses, it could not escape the effects of the general collapse as Hitler's 'Thousand-year Reich' faced extinction. By late January 1945 a renewed Red Army offensive had cleared Poland, and was threatening to engulf Germany from the east.

As one of the few *Jagdgeschwader* remaining on the western front (the majority having been rushed eastwards in a vain attempt to repel the Red tide), JG 27's activities were curtailed by a new OKL directive severely restricting fighter operations in the west. This permitted missions to be flown 'only in those situations promising a real chance of success'. Also, many of the *Geschwader's* ground personnel were now being transferred to infantry duties. Despite these limitations, JG 27 would continue to fight on, suffering a further 150+ casualties (over two-thirds of whom were killed or posted missing) and claiming a final 92 victories during the closing weeks of the war.

On 28 January Leutnant Fritz Gromotka, one of the *Geschwader's* long-serving NCO pilots, now commissioned and soon to be appointed the last *Kapitän* of 9. *Staffel*, was awarded the Knight's Cross. And four days later Oberleutnant Ernst-Wilhelm Reinert, who had taken over command of IV. *Gruppe* after Hanns-Heinz Dudeck failed to return from *Bodenplatte*, finally received his Swords – some six months and two kills behind a no doubt relieved Johannes Steinhoff!

Although the bulk of the *Geschwader* had long been made up of inadequately trained youngsters, it was held together by a core of experienced, long-serving NCOs, many of whom were commissioned during the latter stages of the war – men such as Fritz Gromotka, who had been a member of II. *Gruppe* back in the days of the *Blitzkrieg* against France (see picture on page 27). Recently promoted to Leutnant, Gromotka was appointed *Staffelkapitän* of 9./JG 27 on 1 February 1945. Just visible on his left sleeve is a campaign cuff-band. This bore the legend *AFRIKA*, flanked on each side by a palm tree. Everyone who had been decorated while serving in North Africa was eligible to wear this cuff-title

The *Geschwader's* last Knight's Cross of all went, perhaps fittingly, to the 40-year-old *Kommandeur* of III./JG 27, Hauptmann Dr Peter Werfft, on 22 February 1945. One of the oldest operational fighter pilots in the Luftwaffe, Dr Werfft had scored his first kill over Sevenoaks during the Battle of Britain. Wounded six times since, his final total stood at 26, and included 12 'heavies'.

Three days after *Kommandeur* Dr Werfft's award, his *Gruppe* shot down five P-38s and a single 'Auster' (the latter more likely a US L-4 Grasshopper) in the Cologne area at the expense of one pilot wounded. Such 'Austers' appeared quite regularly among the closing entries on the *Geschwader's* scoreboards. Indeed, five of I./JG 27's last eleven kills were described thus, and 'Austers' (i.e. artillery spotters) accounted for a quarter of III. *Gruppe's* final 24 victories. But, at the other end of the scale, JG 27's pilots were also still claiming some of the finest fighters in the Allies' armoury, including P-51s, Spitfires and Tempests.

Despite their best efforts, however, so overwhelming was the enemy's air superiority over north-west Germany by mid-March 1945 that all four *Gruppen* were ordered to retire from their bases in the Osnabrück region and withdraw eastwards nearer to the centre of the rapidly shrink-

During March 1945 the *Geschwader* reported a total of 47 pilots killed or missing. Only one, 1. *Staffel's* Unteroffizier Hermann Rein, was lost on 17 March. Such were the chaotic conditions in those closing weeks of the war that he had simply disappeared without trace. It was not until this photograph of a cross, bearing his name, came to light in post-war years that the circumstances surrounding his loss were revealed. It was then discovered that his K-4, parts of which were used to decorate the spot where he was buried, had been hit by anti-aircraft fire while carrying out a low-level attack on British troops preparing to cross the Rhine near Wesel

ing Reich. During the third week of March *Stab*, I., II. and III./JG 27 departed Rheine, Hopsten and Hesepe as instructed. But fate overtook Hauptmann Reinert's IV. *Gruppe* before it could evacuate Achmer.

In what was to be the *Gruppe's* last action, Reinert's pilots had clashed with a large formation of P-51s near Osnabrück on 19 March. They managed to bring down just one of the Mustangs, but themselves suffered five killed and six wounded. Two days later the Eighth Air Force mounted heavy raids on JG 27's known bases. Those units at Rheine, Hopsten and Hesepe had flown the coop only hours earlier. But the 180 B-24s which targeted Achmer, and the strafing by fighters which followed, destroyed all but one of IV./JG 27's 38 remaining fighters.

Although few, if any, lives were lost in the raid, it was considered impracticable to re-equip the *Gruppe* amid the chaos that was Germany in the last six weeks of the war. At the end of March IV./JG 27 was therefore officially disbanded.

Meanwhile, the other *Gruppen* fought on. On 24 March III./JG 27 had likewise claimed a single Mustang, but at an even heavier cost of eight pilots killed and one wounded. On that same day I. *Gruppe* lost four of its K-4s together with their pilots. Twenty-four hours later it was the turn of II./JG 27 to report four pilots killed or missing. But during the course of the scrappy dogfight around Bocholt, north of the Ruhr, two P-47s and a Tempest had also gone down. On 7 April II. *Gruppe* was even more successful, accounting for a P-38, two P-47s and a trio of B-26s near Göttingen without loss.

The following week was to see the final parting of the ways. *Stab* and II./JG 27 retired further eastwards to Rathenow, near Berlin, before heading north for the Baltic. While at Schwerin during the latter half of April II. *Gruppe* encountered the Red Air Force for the first time since the opening days of *Barbarossa*. And while able to add ten more Soviet aircraft to the 42 claimed during that single week four years earlier, the price this time was not just one pilot brought down by ground fire, but two killed, one missing and a fourth who disappeared into Russian captivity.

On 30 April Feldwebel Horst Rippert of 7. *Staffel* was credited with II./JG 27's – and, in fact, the *Geschwader's* – last two victories of all.

119

Photographs of aircraft of JG 27 at war's end are notoriously hard to find – and even harder to identify. It has been suggested that this K-4, sitting among the wreckage at Prague-Kbely in May 1945, is 'White 9' of I./JG 27. Despite the suspiciously dark tone of the aft fuselage band, this may well be the case, for Kbely was the last stop for both I. and III. *Gruppen* on their journey south from the Berlin area into Bavaria, and then on to ultimate surrender in Austria. As such, this picture serves as a fitting, if melancholy, tribute to one of the most famous of all *Jagdgeschwader*

Identified as Spitfires, they were almost certainly the two Tempests of No 3 Sqn (old adversaries of JG 27) which failed to return to base after an attack on Schwerin airfield on that date. Shortly after the attackers departed, *Stab* and II. *Gruppe* took off for one last move – to Leck, in Schleswig-Holstein, to await the arrival of the British, and ultimate surrender.

Meanwhile, mid-April 1945 had seen I. and III./JG 27's transfer to Grossenhain, south of Berlin. While here the two *Gruppen* achieved their final kills, with I./JG 27 claiming a pair of (possibly Canadian) Spitfires on 19 April and II./JG 27 destroying another 48 hours later. During the third week of April both *Gruppen* then staged further south still, via Czechoslovakia, to Bad Aibling, in Bavaria. By month's end they had suffered seven more casualties. They would be the last.

It was obvious that the end of the war was now only days away. The two *Gruppenkommandeure*, Hauptleute Emil Clade and Dr Peter Werfft, both veterans of the desert, decided to act on their own initiative. On 2 May they led their *Gruppen* to Salzburg, in Austria, a collecting point for Luftwaffe units in the southern half of a Reich now divided in two by the link-up of US and Soviet forces along the River Elbe.

At Salzburg, however, they simply left their fighters standing among the general confusion and, without any higher authority, instructed the two *Gruppen's* combined personnel, pilots and groundcrew alike – some 1000 men in all – to form a column and march to Saalbach by road.

This they managed to do, despite interference from some die-hard SS units questioning their lack of movement orders. And thus it came about that the history of *Jagdgeschwader* 27, a unit synonymous with the burning sands of North Africa, ended in surrender to the Americans in a small resort town over 3300 ft (1000 m) up in the Austrian Alps.

APPENDICES

APPENDIX 1

COMMANDING OFFICERS

Kommodores of Jagdgeschwader 27 'Afrika'

Ibel, *Oberst* Max	1/10/39	to 10/10/40
Woldenga, *Maj* Bernhard*	11/10/40	to 22/10/40
Schellmann, *Maj* Wolfgang	22/10/40	to 21/6/41 (+)
Woldenga, *Obstlt* Bernhard	21/6/41	to 10/6/42
Neumann, *Obstlt* Eduard	10/6/42	to 22/4/43
Rödel, *Oberst* Gustav	22/4/43	to 29/12/44
Franzisket, *Maj* Ludwig	30/12/44	to 8/5/45

Gruppenkommandeure

I./JG 27

Riegel, *Hptm* Helmut	1/10/39	to 20/7/40 (+)
Neumann, *Maj* Eduard	20/7/40	to 10/6/42
Homuth, *Hptm* Gerhard	10/6/42	to 11/11/42
Setz, *Hptm* Heinrich	12/11/42	to 13/3/43 (+)
Heinecke, *Hptm* Hans-Joachim*	17/3/43	to 7/4/43
Hohagen, *Hptm* Erich	7/4/43	to 1/6/43 WIA
Remmer, *Olt* Hans*	1/6/43	to 15/7/43
Franzisket, *Hptm* Ludwig	15/7/43	to 12/5/44 WIA
Remmer, *Hptm* Hans*	3/44	to 2/4/44 (+)
Blume, *Hptm* Walter*	3/4/44	to 12/5/44
Börngen, *Hptm* Ernst	13/5/44	to 19/5/44 WIA
Redlich, *Maj* Karl-Wolfgang	19/5/44	to 29/5/44 (+)
Blume, *Hptm* Walter	29/5/44	to 11/6/44
Sinner, *Hptm* Rudolf	12/6/44	to 30/7/44
Luckenbach, *Hptm* Siegfried*	30/7/44	to 15/8/44
von Eichel-Streiber, *Hptm* Diethelm	25/8/44	to 30/11/44
Neumeyer, *Hptm* Johannes	1/12/44	to 11/12/44 (+)
Schüller, *Hptm**	11/12/44	to 22/12/44
Schade, *Hptm* Eberhard	22/12/44	to 1/3/45 (+)
Buchholz, *Lt**	1/3/45	to 3/4/45
Clade, *Hptm* Emil	3/4/45	to 8/5/45

II./JG 27

von Schelle, *Hptm* Erich	1/1/40	to 31/1/40
Andres, *Hptm* Werner	1/2/40	to 30/9/40
Düllberg, *Olt* Ernst*	8/8/40	to 4/9/40
Lippert, *Hptm* Wolfgang*	4/9/40	to 30/9/40
Lippert, *Hptm* Wolfgang	1/10/40	to 23/11/41 PoW

Rödel, *Olt* Gustav	23/11/41	to 25/12/41
Gerlitz, *Hptm* Erich	25/12/41	to 20/5/42
Rödel, *Hptm* Gustav	20/5/42	to 20/4/43
Schroer, *Maj* Werner	20/4/43	to 13/3/44
Keller, *Hptm* Fritz	14/3/44	to 12/44
Spies, *Maj* Walter	12/44	to 12/12/44 (+)
Keller, *Hptm* Fritz	12/12/44	to 17/12/44 WIA
Kutscha, *Hptm* Herbert	12/44	to 25/12/44 WIA
Wöffen, *Olt* Anton*	3/1/45	to 20/1/45
Hoyer, *Hptm* Gerhard	21/1/45	to 21/1/45 KAS
Wöffen, *Olt* Anton*	22/1/45	to 1/45
Keller, *Hptm* Fritz	1/45	to 8/5/45

III./JG 27 (Ex-I./JG 131, I./JG 130, I./JG 1)

Woldenga, *Maj* Bernhard	1/4/37	to 13/2/40
Schlichting, *Hptm* Joachim	13/2/40	to 6/9/40 PoW
Dobislav, *Hptm* Max	7/9/40	to 30/9/41
Braune, *Hptm* Erhard	1/10/41	to 11/10/42
Düllberg, *Hptm* Ernst	11/10/42	to 30/9/44
Stigler, *Olt* Franz*	1/10/44	to 7/10/44
Werfft, *Hptm* Dr. Peter	10/44	to 8/5/45
Clade, *Olt* Emil*	2/45	to 3/4/45

IV./JG 27

Sinner, *Hptm* Rudolf	25/5/43	to 13/9/43
Boesler, *Olt* Dietrich*	9/43	to 10/10/43 (+)
Burk, *Olt* Alfred*	10/43	to 18/10/43
Kirschner, *Hptm* Joachim	19/10/43	to 17/12/43 (+)
Meyer, *Hptm* Otto	12/43	to 12/7/44 MIA
Dudeck, *Hptm* Hanns-Heinz	7/44	to 1/1/45 PoW
Reinert, *Hptm* Ernst-Wilhelm	2/1/45	to 23/3/45

Key

*	– acting
(+)	– Killed In Action
MIA	– Missing in Action
WIA	– Wounded in Action
KAS	– Killed on Active Service
PoW	– Prisoner of War

APPENDIX 2

AWARD WINNERS

All JG 27 winners of the Knight's Cross, and its higher grades, are presented here chronologically, with their scores at the time of the award(s) noted in brackets

	Knight's Cross		Oak Leaves		Swords	Fate
Balthasar, *Hptm* Wilhelm	14/6/40	(23)				
Ibel, *Oberst* Max	22/8/40	(0)				
Lippert, *Hptm* Wolfgang	24/9/40	(12)				DAS
Schlichting, *Hptm* Joachim	14/12/40	(3)				POW
Homuth, *Olt* Gerhard	14/6/41	(22)				
Rödel, *Olt/Maj* Gustav	22/6/41	(20)	20/6/43	(78)		
Woldenga, *Maj* Bernhard	5/7/41	(1)				
Redlich, *Olt* Karl-Wolfgang	9/7/41	(21)				KIA
Franzisket, *Olt* Ludwig	20/7/41	(22)				
Von Kageneck, *Olt* Erbo *Graf*	30/7/41	(37)	26/10/41	(65)		DAS
Marseille, *Lt/Olt* Hans-Joachim*	22/2/42	(50)	6/6/42	(75)	18/6/42 (101)	KIA
Schulz, *Ofw* Otto	22/4/42	(44)				MIA
Stahlschmidt, *Lt/Olt* Hans-Arnold	20/8/42	(47)	3/1/44	(59) P		MIA
Körner, *Lt* Friedrich	6/9/42	(36)				PoW
Schroer, *Lt/Hptm* Werner	20/10/42	(49)	2/8/43	(84)		
Steinhausen, *Fw* Günther	3/11/42	(40) P				KIA
Bendert, *Lt* Karl-Heinz	30/12/42	(42)				
Ettel, *Olt* Wolf			31/8/43	(124) P		KIA
Kientsch, *Lt/Olt* Willy	22/11/43	(43)	20/7/44	(52) P		KIA
Remmer, *Hptm* Hans	30/6/44	(26) P				KIA
Börngen, *Maj* Ernst	3/8/44	(38)				
Düllberg, *Maj* Ernst	20/8/44	(37)				
Gromotka, *Lt* Fritz	28/1/45	(29)				
Reinert, *Olt* Ernst-Wilhelm					1/2/45 (174)	
Schramm, *Hptm* Herbert					1/2/45 (42) P	KIA
Werfft, *Hptm* Dr Peter	22/2/45	(26)				

Key

* – Hauptmann Hans-Joachim Marseille was the only member of JG 27 to receive the Diamonds, awarded 2/9/42 for 126 kills

P – Posthumous

DAS – Died on Active Service

APPENDIX 3

SCORES

Unit	Score	Unit Losses (Killed or Missing, all causes)
Stab JG 27	82	12
I./JG 27	989	180
II./JG 27	962	234
III./JG 27	851	173
IV./JG 27	258	126
Totals:	**3142**	**725**

COLOUR PLATES

APPENDICES

1

Ar 68F 'White Double Chevron' of Hauptmann Bernhard Woldenga, Gruppenkommandeur I./JG 131, Jesau, December 1937

Illustrating the simplicity and effectiveness of the Luftwaffe's biplane fighter markings, the white double chevron on the forward fuselage of this Arado indicates that it is the machine of a Gruppenkommandeur. The distinctive black trim on the nose and dorsal spine identifies the unit as JG 131. A combination of geometric symbols and numerals likewise enabled the identity of every other aircraft in the Gruppe to be established at a glance (see photographs in chapter one).

2

Bf 109D-1 'Black Chevron and Flash' of Gruppenstab I./JG 131, Jesau, September 1938

Depicted at the time of the Munich Crisis, one of I./JG 131's recently delivered Doras provides a good example of the anonymity which descended upon the fighter arm with the advent of the Bf 109 – no more coloured trim, just functional drab green overall. Only the Gruppe badge reveals the unit's identity to those in the know. The unusual markings indicate this to be the aircraft officially assigned to the Gruppe's NO (Signals Officer). But as this worthy was an elderly non-flyer, this machine was available to any member of the Gruppenstab as occasion demanded.

3

Bf 109E-3 'Yellow 7' of 3./JG 27, Münster-Handorf, October 1939

If a unit did not have an identifying badge, as is the case here, then the cloak of anonymity was near absolute. This could be a machine of almost any 3. Staffel in the opening weeks of the war, were it not for that tell-tale individual number '7'. I./JG 27 applied this numeral in the continental fashion, i.e. with a small horizontal crossbar at mid-height. Note the large underwing crosses worn by many Luftwaffe aircraft after the ground-to-air recognition problems experienced in Poland.

4

Bf 109E-1 'Red 9' of 2./JG 1, Vörden, December 1939

By the end of 1939 I./JG 1's markings were in a state of transition. 'Red 9' combines a post-Poland enlarged cross underwing with new-style fuselage Balkenkreuz, yet retains the tail swastika centred on the rudder hinge line. But the most obvious innovation is the relocation of the individual aircraft numeral on to the engine cowling. I./JG 1 (the later III./JG 27) was the only Jagdgruppe to display its numerals in this position. Note also 2. Staffel's red spinner trim and short-lived badge (a sword slicing Chamberlain's umbrella in two).

5

Bf 109E-3 'Black 11' of 5./JG 27, Magdeburg, January 1940

When II./JG 27 was activated in January 1940 its Emils were delivered in the new high-demarcation hellblau finish, complete with large fuselage cross and re-positioned tail swastika. One oddity was that, whereas

4. and 6./JG 27 machines wore regulation white and yellow markings respectively, 5. Staffel initially opted to display its individual aircraft numbers in outline form only. The unit's red colour coding was restricted to just the horizontal bar (indicating II. Gruppe) on the aft fuselage.

6

Bf 109E-1 'Red 1' of Oberleutnant Gerd Framm, Staffelkapitän 2./JG 27, Krefeld, February 1940

By early 1940 I./JG 27's aircraft were also wearing the new hellblau camouflage scheme. The aerial mast pennant and diagonal band aft of the fuselage cross proclaim this to be the machine of 2./JG 27's Staffelkapitän. Each of the 12 fighters of this Staffel had the name of a former German colony (lost at the end of World War 1) painted on its engine cowling. Latterly, these names were reduced in size, and supplemented briefly by a Staffel crest, before both gave way to the well known Gruppe badge (see profile 8).

7

Bf 109E-4 'White 1' of Hauptmann Wilhelm Balthasar, Staffelkapitän 1./JG 1, Monchy-Breton, May 1940

Another Staffelkapitän's machine (note aerial mast pennant), this Emil, Wk-Nr 1486, was an early mount of Wilhelm Balthasar. The last of the 11 kill bars painted on the tailfin represented a No 19 Sqn Spitfire brought down near Calais on 26 May 1940. Unlike Gerd Framm (above), who survived the war with ten victories, Balthasar – having risen to Kommodore of JG 2 – would be killed on 3 July 1941, just 24 hours after being awarded the Oak Leaves for his 40th victory.

8

Bf 109E 'White 10' of 1./JG 27, Charleville, May 1940

Pictured at the height of the Blitzkrieg in the west, 'White 10' sports the new I. Gruppe badge introduced immediately prior to the invasion of the Low Countries and France. Following the colonial theme first introduced by 2. Staffel, it features the heads of a native and a lioness(?), superimposed on a silhouette of Africa. Thought at one time to have been introduced after the Gruppe's arrival in Libya, this prescient and apposite choice of unit emblem was in fact made a good 12 months earlier!

9

Bf 109E 'Yellow 6' of 6./JG 27, Fiennes, September 1940

By the closing stages of the Battle of Britain the previously pristine hellblau flanks of II. Gruppe's Emils had been toned down by applications of camouflage green (anything from a light overspray to dense dapple). This machine also sports the common Channel Front livery of yellow engine cowling and rudder. Note the new Gruppe badge, first introduced in August 1940, featuring the Berlin bear – also the single victory bar on the rudder. This latter could refer to any one of at least four 6. Staffel pilots who claimed their first kill during the Battle.

10

Bf 109E-7 'White 1' of Oberleutnant Wolfgang Redlich, Staffelkapitän 1./JG 27, Guines, September 1940

123

Even more heavily dappled than the machine in profile 9, this aircraft sports the *Gruppe* badge, a *Staffelkapitän's* diagonal stripe and boasts nine kill bars alongside the tail swastika (Redlich's ninth was a Hurricane downed over London on 9 September). Wk-Nr. 5580 also offers a (very tenuous) link to the one theatre of war in which JG 27 played no part – Scandinavia. On 24 February 1942, long after retirement from I./JG 27, it was being ferried, as 'Yellow 25', to a *Jagdgruppe* in Norway when Unteroffizier Anton Hunold lost his bearings and landed wheels-up on a frozen lake in Sweden!

11

Bf 109E-7 'Black 2' of 5./JG 27, Vrba, March 1941
Many II. *Gruppe* machines changed their Channel Front markings to those of the Balkan theatre by the simple expedient of adding yellow wingtips and a narrow band around the aft fuselage. But whereas 4. and 6. *Staffeln* appear to have positioned these bands carefully in the space between the fuselage cross and horizontal bar, 5./JG 27 painted the yellow band directly *over* the latter. Note also the *Staffel's* continuing practice of combining the fighter's individual black numeral with the red *Gruppe* bar (see profile 5).

12

Bf 109E-4/B 'Yellow 5' of 6./JG 27, Vilna, June 1941
In the month separating II. *Gruppe's* return from Greece and the invasion of the Soviet Union, groundcrews obviously found time to apply textbook *Barbarossa* livery of 'bright yellow underwing tips (one-third span) and a broad band aft of the fuselage cross'. This particular machine is fitted with the large ventral pannier carrying 96 SD-2 *Splitterbomben* (see *Osprey Aircraft of the Aces 37 - Bf 109 Aces of the Russian Front*, page 20). Arranged in 24 rows of 4, the bombs' steel arming cables hung in the airstream like a fringe.

13

Bf 109E-7 'Yellow 1' of Oberleutnant Erbo *Graf* von Kageneck, *Staffelkapitän* 9./JG 27, Solzy, August 1941
When I./JG 1 became III./JG 27 in July 1940 it did not introduce a III. *Gruppe* vertical bar on the aft fuselage as laid down in then current Luftwaffe regulations. Presumably the unit's unique practice of displaying its individual aircraft numbers on the engine cowlings was considered sufficient a recognition/identification aid in itself. The last of the 45 victory bars shown here on the rudder represents a Soviet single-engined fighter, logged as an 'I-18' (but probably a MiG-3), shot down near Novgorod on 16 August 1941.

14

Bf 109E-7/trop 'Black Chevron A' of Oberleutnant Ludwig Franzisket, *Gruppen*-Adjutant I./JG 27, Ain-el-Gazala, September 1941
Displaying just half the number of kills of the machine above (23, with the last being a Hurricane east of Sidi Barrani on 9 September 1941), 'Ziskus' Franzisket's tropicalised E-7 wears one of the camouflage schemes first introduced during I./JG 27's early months in the desert (most aircraft having arrived in North Africa in standard temperate finish). The prominent yellow markings would slowly disappear, white being the recognition colour

applied to all Axis aircraft, both German and Italian, in the Mediterranean theatre.

15

Bf 109F-4/trop 'Black Double Chevron' of Hauptmann Eduard Neumann, *Gruppenkommandeur* I./JG 27, Ain-el-Gazala, November 1941
When I. *Gruppe* began to re-equip with *Friedrichs* at the end of 1941 these too initially displayed large areas of yellow paint on engine cowlings and rudders (although no sign of the latter beneath 'Edu' Neumann's current tally of 11 kills). The white theatre markings were restricted to wingtips and aft fuselage band. This machine does, however, provide a good example of the basic camouflage scheme which would be worn by JG 27's aircraft for the remainder of their desert service – overall tan uppersurfaces and light blue undersides.

16

Bf 109F-4/trop 'Black 9' of 5./JG 27, Ain-el-Gazala, December 1941
II. *Gruppe* converted to tropicalised *Friedrichs* while at Döberitz in the autumn of 1941, and prior to its transfer to North Africa. This is one of those original Döberitz machines. The clue? The white theatre band, painted around the rear fuselage after arrival in the Mediterranean, has partly obscured the horizontal II. *Gruppe* bar which had been applied (along with the individual aircraft number) while the unit was still in Germany.

17

Bf 109F-4/trop 'Black 2' of 8./JG 27, Tmimi, December 1941
Likewise a brand-new arrival in Libya after re-equipment at Döberitz, 'Black 2' of III./JG 27 shows that this *Gruppe* chose not to cover up its aft fuselage symbol, but left a gap when subsequently applying the white theatre band. When converting on to the Bf 109F the *Gruppe* had abandoned its practice of displaying its aircraft numbers on the engine cowling. It was this which now necessitated the use of a *Gruppe* identity symbol. But rather than use a standard vertical bar, III./JG 27 opted instead for the 'wavy bar' device dating back to pre-war biplane days.

18

Bf 109F-4/trop 'Yellow 14' of Leutnant Hans-Joachim Marseille, 3./JG 27, Tmimi, May 1942
Undoubtedly the most famous of all desert *Friedrichs* were the succession of 'Yellow 14s' flown by Hans-Joachim Marseille. He used this particular machine, Wk-Nr. 10059, during the early summer months of 1942 (it would be lost in a mid-air collision near El Alamein in September while being piloted as 'Yellow 12' by Leutnant Friedrich Hoffmann). The last three of the 68 kill bars shown here on the rudder were a trio of Kittyhawks claimed near Tobruk on 31 May. Note that few of Marseille's aircraft wore the I. *Gruppe* badge (for other examples see *Osprey Aircraft of the Aces 2 - Bf 109 Aces of North Africa and the Mediterranean*).

19

Bf 109F-4/trop 'Red 1' of Leutnant Hans-Arnold Stahlschmidt, *Staffelkapitän* 2./JG 27, Quotaifiya, August 1942

Although overshadowed by his close friend Marseille, 'Fifi' Stahlschmidt was another of I./JG 27's highly successful desert *Experten*. The 48 kill bars adorning the rudder of his 'Red 1' – all of them victories scored in North Africa – had already won him the Knight's Cross. But his promising career was brought to an end when he was reported missing (in 'Red 4') south-east of El Alamein on 7 September 1942. Note that this particular *Friedrich*, unlike the four immediately before it in the colour section, wears the alternative camouflage scheme, with the demarcation line between the uppersurface tan and light blue undersides positioned much lower on the fuselage.

20

Bf 109F-4/trop 'Yellow 5' of Leutnant Gerhard Mix, 6./JG 27, Quotaifiya, August 1942
At the other end of the scale to Marseille and Stahlschmidt, 6. *Staffel's* Gerhard Mix did not (as far as is known) achieve a single victory before being forced to belly-land behind Allied lines on 14 August 1942. His 'Yellow 5' is included to show the unusual style of fuselage cross with its enlarged black centre field and no outer edging. Although seen on several of JG 27's machines, this was not a unit modification, for similar crosses also appeared on *Friedrichs* of neighbouring III./JG 53. Possibly applied at one of the air depots in Italy, the reason for this deviation from the standard *Balkenkreuz* remains unknown.

21

Bf 109G-4/trop 'White 7' of 4./JG 27, Trapani, May 1943
Having left all of its tan-camouflaged machines in North Africa, II./JG 27's new complement of *Gustavs* were delivered in factory standard grey schemes, to which were added the regulation white Mediterranean theatre markings. 'White 7', displaying both *Gruppe* and *Staffel* badges, is typical of the aircraft which bore the brunt of the overwater Sicily-Tunisia convoy escort duties during the spring of 1943.

22

Bf 109G-4/R6 'White 10' of 1./JG 27, Poix, May 1943
Meanwhile, I. *Gruppe* had returned to north-west France, where, to keep in line with the resident JGs 2 and 26, its new *Gustavs* were given standard mid-war Channel Front recognition markings of yellow rudders and lower engine cowlings. Note the retention of I./JG 27's *'Afrika'* badge, now again as geographically inappropriate as it was when the unit was last in the area during the Battle of Britain in the summer of 1940.

23

Bf 109G-6/trop 'Yellow 1' of Oberleutnant Dietrich Boesler, *Staffelkapitän* 12./JG 27, Tanagra, July 1943
When IV./JG 27 was activated in Greece in the spring of 1943, it was unable to use the 'wavy bar' which had by that time become the official marking for IV. *Gruppe* (III./JG 27 having already 'appropriated' the said symbol). The new unit therefore introduced its unique 'double horizontal bar' device depicted here. Note also the distinctive spiral spinner and *Staffelkapitän's* circular 'pennant' on the aerial mast. Dietrich Boesler scored a single kill – a Spitfire off Kós on 19 September – before himself falling victim to B-17s the following month.

24

Bf 109G-6/R6 'Red 13' of Feldwebel Heinrich Bartels, 11./JG 27, Kalamaki, November 1943
By the late autumn of 1943, IV. /JG 27's G-6 'gunboats' were wearing regulation 'wavy bar' IV. *Gruppe* markings, as witness here 'Red 13', the mount of the unit's most successful pilot, Heinrich Bartels. The elaborate rudder decoration, topped by a representation of the Knight's Cross (awarded a year earlier for 45 victories) shows exactly 70 kill bars, the last four a quartet of P-38s claimed near Kalamaki on 17 November. Note the name of Bartels' wife, Marga, below the windscreen. This reportedly featured on every machine he flew.

25

Bf 109G-6/R6 trop 'White 9' of 7./JG 27, Máleme, December 1943
The reason IV./JG 27 was at last able to sport its 'proper' *Gruppe* symbol is that III./JG 27 had been persuaded (for 'persuaded' read ordered?) to discontinue its use of this marking during a recent round of re-equipment. In its place, III. *Gruppe's Gustavs* now carried a regulation vertical bar aft of the fuselage cross. In addition, 'White 9' wears both *Gruppe* and *Staffel* badges, the latter also newly introduced. The all-white tailfin and rudder indicates the machine of a formation leader, possibly that of *Staffelkapitän* Emil Clade.

26

Bf 109G-6/R6 'White 4' of 1./JG 27, Fels am Wagram, January 1944
Having transferred from north-west to south-east Europe in the late summer of 1943, it was at Fels am Wagram in January 1944 that I. *Gruppe* first began to wear the sage-green aft fuselage bands indicating the unit's incorporation into the growing Defence of the Reich organisation. Note, however, that 'White 4' still sports the *Gruppe* badge, as well as a yellow undercowling and rudder, the latter markings introduced during I./JG 27's earlier seven-month stint in northern Europe.

27

Bf 109G-6/R6 'White 23' of 1./JG 27, Fels am Wagram, January 1944
For a period at Wels I./JG 27's strength was increased to almost double its normal establishment. This was to enable the *Gruppe* to perform an additional function – the training of experienced pilots from other units to become formation leaders. Hence the two numerals carried by this 'gunboat'. 'White 23' (the high number a reflection of the unit's increased size) was its *Staffel* identity, 'Black 1' its code for training purposes. The latter has necessitated the removal of the *Gruppe* badge. But many such identifying emblems were disappearing by this late stage of the war anyway, and soon the famous *'Afrika'* motif – worn for nearly four years – would be no more.

28

Bf 109G-6/R6 'Yellow 8' of 12./JG 27, Skopje, February 1944
After transferring from Greece northwards into Yugoslavia, IV./JG 27 dispensed with the white aft fuselage bands of the Mediterranean theatre. But although now engaged primarily against US heavy bombers attacking

south-east Europe, it was not yet officially part of the homeland defence organisation, and so displayed no green identity band either. Note the white spiralled spinner and white rudder, this latter possibly indicating the machine of a *Schwarmführer*.

29

Bf 109G-6/R6 'Black 2' of 5./JG 27, Wiesbaden-Erbenheim, February 1944

More surprisingly, perhaps, II./JG 27, based in central Germany, and therefore in the thick of Defence of the Reich operations, was not yet wearing the *Geschwader's* sage-green identifying bands either. This heavily-dappled *Gustav* does, however, still sport the *Gruppe* badge. And note the unit's preference for more tightly spiralled spinners. This may have been the machine Leutnant Heinz Schlechter was flying when he rammed a B-17 over the *Gruppe's* Merzhausen base on 12 May 1944 (the third of his four reported victories).

30

Bf 109G-6/R6 'Black Double Chevron' of Hauptmann Otto Meyer, *Gruppenkommandeur* IV./JG 27, Graz-Thalerhof, March 1944

Another of IV. *Gruppe's* increasingly anonymous machines, *Kommandeur* Otto Meyer at least ensured that, at unit level, his pilots could instantly recognise their leader – look at the size of those chevrons! Otto Meyer would be reported missing over the Invasion front on 12 July 1944, the victim of either Allied fighters or anti-aircraft fire. 15 of his 21 victories had been scored while serving with JG 27.

31

Bf 109G-6/R6 trop 'White 3' of Unteroffizier Franz Stadler, 7./JG 27, Máleme, April 1944

The last chapter in JG 27's three-year long association with the Mediterranean theatre was written by 7. *Staffel*, which was still operating its tropicalised *Gustavs* from north-western Crete when every other unit of the *Geschwader* was already engaged in defending the homeland. Unteroffizier Stadler claimed the last of the six SM.84 transports downed north-east of Brindisi on 14 May 1944 (see text). He must therefore be credited with the very last of all the *Geschwader's* 1740 Mediterranean kills. It was his one and only victory.

32

Bf 109G-6 'White 5' of 7./JG 27, Connantre, June 1944

Little more than a month after its Cretan successes, 7. *Staffel* rejoined the rest of III. *Gruppe* and was thrown into action over the Normandy invasion front. In the interim, presumably during the *Staffel's* brief stop-over at Wien (Vienna)-Götzendorf, it had found time to re-equip with non-tropicalised, late-model *Gustavs* (note the tall tail), which now bore JG 27's sage-green Defence of the Reich band around the rear fuselage aft of the *Gruppe's* vertical bar.

33

Bf 109G-6/AS 'Yellow 2' of 6./JG 27, Fels am Wagram, July 1944

While I., III. and IV. *Gruppen* were involved over Normandy, II./JG 27 was down in Austria busy working up on its new G-6/AS high-altitude fighters. These also now wore the *Geschwader's* green Defence of the Reich band. But note the difference in location of the band between II. *Gruppe* (immediately aft of the *Balkenkreuz*) and III. *Gruppe* (seen in profile 32), and the narrowness of the width of both when compared to I./JG 27's broad rear fuselage markings (profiles 26 and 27). The yellow underwing tip indicates that the pilot of this machine is experienced in blind-flying. The *Gruppe's* younger pilots were ordered to formate on such aircraft in conditions of poor visibility.

34

Bf 109G-14 'White 14' of Oberleutnant Ernst-Georg Altnorthoff, *Staffelkapitän* 13./JG 27, Hustedt, September 1944

Pictured after the depredations of the Normandy campaign, this is one of the 68 brand-new G-14s delivered to IV. *Gruppe* while resting and re-equipping in northern Germany. Still upholding IV.JG 27's seeming preference for anonymity, it is not known whether the *Geschwader's* identifying sage-green homeland defence bands had been applied to the *Gruppe's* machines by the time it resumed operations in October. The first eight of Altnorthoff's eleven kills were achieved with IV./JG 27 before the unit's disbandment in March 1945 (and the final three with another unit the following month).

35

Bf 109G-14/AS 'Blue 11' (Wk-Nr. 785750) of 8./JG 27, Rheine-Hopsten, March 1945

Pictured as hostilities drew towards a close, 'Blue 11' is typical of II./JG 27's late-war equipment. Note that the sage-green band still abuts directly on to the fuselage cross. Other, more general, features common to late-production Bf 109s are the prominent display of the Werk-Nummer (in this instance, the 'last four' carried above the horizontal *Gruppe* bar) and the sharply defined dapple of the tail unit.

36

Bf 109K-4 'Red 18' of 2./JG 27, Bad Aibling, April 1945

Reconstructed from photographs of wreckage, this depiction of 2. *Staffel's* 'Red 18' is representative of I./JG 27's machines in the closing weeks of the war. Note that this *Gruppe's* broad aft fuselage band was also apparently retained until the very end.

37

Bf 109K-4 'Blue 7' of 12./JG 27, Prague-Kbely, April 1945

By contrast, this K-4 of III. *Gruppe*, sporting another typical late-war camouflage scheme, indicates that the application of III./JG 27's Defence of the Reich bands had undergone a minor change. They were now broader than before (although still not quite of I./JG 27 dimensions), with the *Gruppe's* vertical bar superimposed.

38

Gotha Go 145A 'SM+NQ' of *Stab* JG 27, Cherbourg, August 1940

Like every other *Jagdgeschwader*, JG 27 had its complement of station 'hacks' and general runabouts. This Gotha biplane, assigned directly to the *Geschwaderstab*, did not last long, however. Engaged on a mail run from the Channel Islands back to Strasbourg on 28 August 1940 – the height of the Battle of Britain, and the day of the *Stab's* transfer from Cherbourg to Guines – pilot Unteroffizier Leonhard Buckle lost his bearings and landed inadvertently, and intact, on Lewes racecourse in Sussex. As the RAF's BV207, Gotha Wk-Nr. 1115 went on to perform sterling service 'under new management'!

39
Bf 108B 'TI+EY' of I./JG 27, Graz-Thalerhof, April 1941
A much more luxurious 'bird', with enclosed cabin for pilot and three passengers, this immaculate *Taifun* allowed Hauptmann Eduard Neumann and his *Gruppenstab* I./JG 27 to travel in some style. They were soon to be deprived of its comforts, however, for 'TI+EY' reportedly remained behind when the *Gruppe's Emils* left for Africa later that same month. Sister ship 'TI+EN' of the *Geschwaderstab* did make it across the Mediterranean, only to be blown up during the retreat from El Alamein in November 1942.

40
Fi 156C-3 'DO+AI' of *Stab* JG 27, Quotaifiya, July 1942
Another *Geschwaderstab* runabout to make it to Africa was this tan-camouflaged *Storch*, complete with Mediterranean theatre markings and Oberstleutnant Woldenga's recently introduced *Geschwader* badge. Hardly in the 'luxury' class, Fi 156 Wk-Nr. 5407 was a true maid-of-all-work, not only undertaking vital communications and liaison duties, but also retrieving downed pilots from the tractless wastes of the Libyan and Egyptian deserts. Her career was brought to an end by an Allied bombing raid on Quotaifiya on 8 August 1942.

SELECTED BIBLIOGRAPHY

BEER, SIEGFRIED and KARNER, STEFAN, *Der Krieg aus der Luft, Kärnten und Steiermark 1941-1945*. Weishaupt Verlag, Graz, 1992

BROOKES, ANDREW, *Air War over Italy, 1943-1945*. Ian Allan, Shepperton, 2000

CONSTABLE, TREVOR J and TOLIVER, COL RAYMOND F, *Horrido! Fighter Aces of the Luftwaffe*. Macmillan, New York, 1968

CULL, BRIAN et al, *Twelve Days in May: The Air Battle for Northern France and the Low Countries 10-21 May 1940*. Grub Street, London, 1995

FREEMAN, ROGER A, *Mighty Eighth War Diary*. Janes, London, 1981

GIRBIG, WERNER, *Start im Morgengrauen*. Motorbuch Verlag, Stuttgart, 1973

GIRBIG, WERNER, *.. mit Kurs auf Leuna*. Motorbuch Verlag, Stuttgart, 1980

OBERMAIER, ERNST, *Die Ritterkreuzträger der Luftwaffe 1939-1945: Band I, Jagdflieger*. Verlag Dieter Hoffmann, Mainz, 1966

PRIEN, JOCHEN et al, *Messerschmitt Bf 109 im Einsatz beim JG 27* (3 vols of individual *Gruppe* Histories). Struve-Druck, Eutin

RAMSEY, WINSTON G (ed), *The Battle of Britain Then and Now*. After the Battle, London, 1985

RING, HANS and GIRBIG, WERNER, *Jagdgeschwader 27*. Motorbuch Verlag, Stuttgart, 1971

RUST, KENN C, *Fifteenth Air Force Story*. Historical Aviation Album, Temple City, 1976

SHORES, CHRISTOPHER and RING, HANS, *Fighters over the Desert*. Neville Spearman, London, 1969

SHORES, CHRISTOPHER et al, *Fighters over Tunisia*. Neville Spearman, London, 1975

SHORES, CHRISTOPHER et al, *Air War for Yugoslavia, Greece and Crete 1940-41*. Grub Street, London, 1987

SHORES, CHRISTOPHER et al, *Fledgling Eagles*. Grub Street, London, 1991

SMITH, PETER and WALKER, EDWIN, *War in the Aegean*. William Kimber, London, 1974

ULRICH, JOHANN, *Der Luftkrieg über Österreich 1939-1945*. Heeresgeschichtliches Museum, Vienna

INDEX

References to illustrations are shown in **bold**.
Plates are shown with page and caption locators in brackets.

Adolph, Oberleutnant Walter 13, 20
Afrika Korps 80, 82, 90, 92
air-sea rescue (ASR) service 29
Altnorthoff, Oberleutnant Ernst-Georg **34**(60, 126), **97**
Andres, Hauptmann Werner 16, 31, 39
Ankum-Frank, Hauptmann Albrecht von 31
Arado Ar 68F **7**, 7, **8**, 8, **1**(52, 123)
Arnold, Feldwebel Ernst **34**
Austria 104-106, 109-110, 120

Balkans 42-47, 100-102, 110
Balthasar, Hauptmann Wilhelm 20, 23, 24, **25**, 25, **26**, 26, 33, **7**(53, 123)
Bartels, Feldwebel (later Oberfeldwebel) Heinrich **24**(57, 125), **100**, 100-101, **101**, 110, 112, 116
Beushausen, Oberfeldwebel Heinz 30
Blazytko, Oberfeldwebel Franz 50
Bode, Oberleutnant Günther **36**
Boesler, Oberleutnant Dietrich **23**(57, 125), 96, 98, 100
Börngren, Hauptmann Ernst 94, **108**, 108
Braune, Hauptmann (later Oberleutnant) Erhard 'Jack' 33, 78, **81**, **82**, 88
Braxator, Leutnant Horst 23
Bristol Blenheim **45**
Bristol Bombay **4**
Buckle, Unteroffizier Leonhard 34, 126-127
Burk, Oberleutnant Alfred **97**, 97, 100

Clade, Oberfeldwebel (later Leutnant) Emil **4**, 20, 84, 85, **98**, 120
Crete 78-79
Curtiss Tomahawk **81**

Dettmann, Oberleutnant Fritz **104**, **105**
Dobislav, Oberleutnant (later Hauptmann) Max 8, 35, **45**, 45
Dudeck, Hauptmann Hanns-Heinz **111**, 112, 117
Düllberg, Hauptmann (later Major) Ernst 84, 88, **101**, 110, 112, 113

El Alamein 82, 88-89
Espenlaub, Feldwebel (later Oberfeldwebel) Albert **65**, **74**, 74
Ettel, Oberleutnant Wolf 96, **97**, 97

Fenzl, Leutnant Helmuth **88**
Fiat CR.42: **33**
Fieseler Fi 156C-3: **40**(61, 127)
Fischer, Oberleutnant Karl **38**
Fliegerführer z.b.V. 18
Fliegerkorps, VIII. 22, 27-28, 33, 43, 47
Förster, Oberfeldwebel Hermann 74
Framm, Oberleutnant Gerd **21**, **6**(53, 123)
France 22-40, 103-104, 111-112, 114
Franzisket, Leutnant (later Major) Ludwig 'Ziskus' 20, 29, **14**(55, 124), 67, 68, **69**, 73, 76, **107**, 116

Galland, Hauptmann Adolf 15-16, 21, 22, 25
Gazala, Battle of 80-81
Geisler, General Hans **78**
Gerlach, Hauptmann Hans-Joachim **42**, 44
Gerlitz, Hauptmann Erich **68**, **78**, 79-80
Geschwaderstab JG 27: 12, **27**, 28, 42, 44, **38**, **40**(61, 126-127), 90, 94, 109, 119
Gobert, Hauptmann Ernst-Ascan 115
Göring, *Reichsmarschall* Hermann **87**, 111
Gotha Go 145A **38**(61, 126-127)
Gott, Lt Gen William H E **4**, 84-85
Grimpe, Unteroffizier Friedrich **43**
Gromotka, Unteroffizier (later Leutnant) Fritz **27**, 117, **118**
groundcrew **11**, **43**, **75**, **77**
Gruppen
I./JG 1: 10, **11**, 11, 13, 20, 23, 24, 25, 27, 28, 29
aircraft **16**, **18**, **26**, **29**
I./JG 21: 10, 13
I./JG 27: 12, 17, 28, 38-39, 45, 47, 87, 88-89, 103, 104, 111, 120
aircraft **15**, **17**, **28**, **36**, **46**, **14**, **15**(55, 124), **39**(61, 127), **104**, **107**
II./JG 27: 16-17, 42, 44, 49, 70, 90, 94, 108, 113, 114, 119
aircraft **30**, **31**, **33**, **44**, **93**, **108**
Battle of Britain 31, 39, 40
Battle of France 24-25, 27, 28
III./JG 27: 29, 40, 45, 87-88, 102, 109, 112, 120
aircraft **29**, **41**, **88**, **94**
Balkans 42, 44
Crete 94, 96
Greece 97, 98
IV./JG 27: **30**(59, 126), **96**, 96, 97, **100**, 100, **101**, 101, 109, 110, 119
III./JG 53: 79-80
I./JG 130: 10
I./JG 131: 6-7, 8, 9, 10, **1**(52, 123)
II./JG 132 'Richthofen' 6, 7
I.(J)/LG 2: 15
II.(Schl)/LG 2: 16, **18**, **40**
Gruppenstab I./JG 27: **46**
Gruppenstab II./JG 27: **71**
Gruppenstab I./JG 131: **2**(52, 123)

Hackl, Feldwebel Ernst **97**
Hannak, Oberleutnant Günther 96
Heinecke, Oberleutnant Hans-Joachim 82
Henschel Hs 123: **18**
heraldry **62-63**
Hitler, Adolf 9, 10, 64, 116
Hohagen, Hauptmann Erich **104**
Homuth, Oberleutnant (later Major) Gerhard 20, **21**, 67-68, **68**, **77**, **81**, 81, 88-89

Ibel, Oberstleutnant (later Oberst) Max 12, **13**, 29, 33, 40
Italy 94, 100

Jagdgeschwader
JG 2 'Richthofen' 10
JG 27 'Afrika' 6, 114-115
JG 77: **89**
JG 126 (III./ZG 26) 15
JG 131: 9-10
JG 132 'Richthofen' 9-10
James, Sgt H E **4**, 84-85

Kageneck, Leutnant (later Oberleutnant) Erbo *Graf* von 20, 23-24, 45, 49-50, **50**, **13**(55, 124), 74-75
Kesselring, Generalfeldmarschall Albert **78**, **87**
Kientsch, Leutnant (later Oberleutnant) Willy **91**, 91, 92, 93, 109
Kirschner, Hauptmann Joachim 100, 101, **102**
Körner, Leutnant Friedrich **84**, 84
Kothmann, Leutnant Willi 46
Kübelwagen **83**, **111**

Langanke, Leutnant Gustav-Adolf 49, 72
Lange, Leutnant Heinz 14
Lange, Feldwebel Werner **65**
Larrazábal, *Commandante* Angel Salas 51
Lege, Unteroffizier Paul **39**
Lewes, Leutnant Hans 89, 93
Lippert, Hauptmann Wolfgang **39**, 39-40, **44**, **72**, 72
Luftflotten 10, 12
Luftkreiskommando I (later 1) 6, 9
Luftwaffenkommandos 9, 10

Malta 45, 87, 90
markings 7-8, 9, **62-63**
Marseille, Oberfähnrich (later Hauptmann) Hans-Joachim
aircraft **18**(56, 124), **86**
as Oberfähnrich 41-42, **46**, 46-47, **64**, 67-68
as Leutnant 69-70, **70**, 72-73, 76, **77**, **78**, 78
as Oberleutnant 80, **81**, 81-82, **83**, **85**, 85-87, **87**, 88
McKellar, Flt Lt 'Archie' **39**, 39-40
Messerschmitt
Bf 108B **39**(61, 127)
Bf 109D-1: **2**(52, 123)
Bf 109E **10**, 10, **47**
JG 1: **10**, **14**, **16**, **18**, **23**, **26**, **29**
I./JG 27: **15**, **17**, **28**, **36**
II./JG 27: **30**, **31**, **33**, **44**
III./JG 27: **41**
1./JG 27: **36**, **8**(53, 123), **68**, **70**
2./JG 27: **16**, **37**, **68**, **69**
3./JG 27: **34**, **67**
4./JG 27: **44**
5./JG 27: **4**, **24**, **39**
6./JG 27: **27**, **42**, **9**(54, 123)
7./JG 27: **38**, **43**
8. & 9./JG 27: **45**
II.(Schl.)/LG 2: **40**
Bf 109E-1: **4**(52, 123), **6**(53, 123)
Bf 109E-3: **38**, **3**(52, 123), **5**(53, 123)
Bf 109E-4: **7**(53, 123)
Bf 109E-4/B **12**(54, 124)
Bf 109E-7: **25**, **46**, **10**, **11**, **13**(54, 55, 123-124)
Bf 109E-7/trop **46**, **50**, **14**(55, 124), **64**
Bf 109F 70-71, **74**, **77**, **88**, **89**, **94**
Bf 109F-4/trop **15-20**(55-56, 124-125), **71**, **73**, **79**
Bf 109G **93**, **100**, **107**, **108**
Bf 109G-2/trop 85-86, **95**
Bf 109G-4: **103**
Bf 109G-4/R6: **22**(57, 125)
Bf 109G-4/trop **21**(57, 125)
Bf 109G-6: **32**(59, 126), **97**, **104**, **105**
Bf 109G-6/AS **33**(60, 126), **112**, 113
Bf 109G-6/R6: **24**(57, 125), **26-30**(58-59, 125-126)
Bf 109G-6/R6 trop **25**(58, 125), **31**(59, 126), **98**, **99**
Bf 109G-6/trop **23**(57, 125), **96**
Bf 109G-14: **34**(60, 126)
Bf 109G-14/AS **35**(60, 126)
Bf 109K-4: **36**, **37**(60-61, 126), **120**
Me 323 *Gigant* 92
Mettig, Major Martin 10, 13, 15
Meyer, Hauptmann Otto **30**(59, 126), 101, 102, 110, 112
Mix, Leutnant Gerhard **20**(56, 125)
Montgomery, Gen Bernard Law **4**, 85, 88
Müller, Oberfeldwebel Alfred **112**

Neumann, Hauptmann (later Oberstleutnant) Eduard 'Edu' 92
aircraft **15**(55, 124)
caravan **35**, **80**
as Hauptmann 30, 41-42, **67**, 67, **70**, **78**, **79**
as Major 76, 79, **81**, 81, 87
Neumann, Leutnant (later Oberleutnant) Julius 'Jupp' **27**, **31**, 33
North Africa **66**

Operation
Barbarossa 47-49
Bodenplatte 117
Crusader 72-76
Flax 90-91
Marita 43-47
Paula 25

'Palm Sunday Massacre' 91
Pantellaria 92-93
Panzergruppe von Kleist 22
Philipp, Unteroffizier Rudolf **97**
Potez 63.11: **23**
Pöttgen, Unteroffizier Rainer 46-47
Prussia, East 6-9, 10-12

Redlich, Oberleutnant (later Major) Karl-Wolfgang 'Papa' 20, **10**(54, 123-124), **65**, 66, 67, **68**, 68, 72, 73, 106, 108
Rein, Unteroffizier Hermann **119**
Reinert, Leutnant (later Oberleutnant) Ernst-Wilhelm 110, **111**, 117
Remmer, Hauptmann Hans 105, **107**
Richthofen, Generalmajor Wolfram *Frhr.* von 17, 18
Riegel, Hauptmann Helmut 12, **15**, 22, 30
Rippert, Feldwebel Horst 119-120
Rödel, Leutnant (later Oberst) Gustav 21, **81**, 89, 109, 111-112, **112**, 116
aircraft **44**
as Oberleutnant 44, 49, 71-72, 79, 80
as Major 92, 94, **97**, 99
Rommel, General Erwin 64, 66, **74**, 76, 80, **81**
Rosenboom, Leutnant (later Oberleutnant) Hans-Volkert 13-14, 30

Sawallisch, Oberfeldwebel Erwin 49
Schellmann, Hauptmann (later Major) Wolfgang 40, 43, **48**, 48-49
Scherer, Leutnant Ulrich 30, **34**
Schlang, Oberleutnant Jost 87, 99
Schlichting, Hauptmann Joachim 15, 20, 35, 40
Schmid, Generalleutnant Josef **114**
Schneider, Feldwebel (later Leutnant) Bernd **4**, 85, 90
Schramm, Oberleutnant Herbert 109
Schroer, Leutnant (later Major) Werner 66, **69**, 83, 88, 89, 92, 93, 94-96, **95**, **108**, 109, **110**
Schulz, Unteroffizier Ernst **14**
Schulz, Oberfeldwebel (later Oberleutnant) Otto **71**, 71-72, 76, **78**, 78
Setz, Oberleutnant (later Hauptmann) Heinrich **103**, 103-104
Sicily 90, 92, 94, 96, 97
Sinner, Hauptmann Rudolf 'Rudi' 96, 98
Sippel, Unteroffizier Hans **65**, 66-67
Special Air Service (SAS) 72
Stab see *Geschwaderstab*
Stadler, Unteroffizier Franz **31**(59, 126)
Staffeln
1./JG 1: **18**, **7**(53, 123)
2./JG 1: **23**, **4**(52, 123)
3./JG 1: **14**
1./JG 27: **36**, **8**(53, 123), **10**(54, 123-124), **22**(57, 125), **26**, **27**(58, 125), **65**, **68**, **70**, 72, **73**, **74**, **105**
2./JG 27: **16**, **37**, **6**(53, 123), **19**(56, 124-125), **36**(60, 126), **68**, **69**, **103**
3./JG 27: **34**, **3**(52, 123), **18**(56, 124), **64**, **67**, 72, **75**, **105**
4./JG 27: 17, **44**, **21**(57, 125), **112**
5./JG 27: **4**, 17, **24**, **25**, **38**, **39**, **5**(53, 123), **11**(54, 124), **16**(55, 124), **29**(59, 126), **71**, **79**
6./JG 27: 17, **27**, **42**, **9**(54, 123), **12**(54, 124), **20**(56, 125), **33**, **34**(60, 126), **91**
7./JG 27: **38**, **43**, **25**(58, 125), **31**, **32**(59, 126), 96, **98**, 102
8./JG 27: **45**, **17**(56, 124), **35**(60, 126), **95**, 96
9./JG 27: **45**, **50**, **13**(55, 124), 96
10./JG 27: 79, 85, 96
11./JG 27: **24**(57, 125), 96
12./JG 27: **23**(57, 125), **28**(58, 125-126), **37**(61, 126), 96
15.(*span.*)/JG 27: **51**
2./JG 131: **7**, 9
3./JG 131: **8**, 9
Stahl, Leutnant Werner 29
Stahlschmidt, Oberfeldwebel (later Leutnant) Hans-Arnold 'Fifi' **19**(56, 124-125), **78**, **83**, 83, 84
Steinhausen, Feldwebel (later Leutnant) Günther **65**, 83
Steinhoff, Oberleutnant Johannes 'Mäcki' 41, 42, 110
Strobl, Leutnant Helmut **25**
Stückler, Feldwebel Alfred **95**

Tobruk 66, 68, 73, 82
Trützschler-d'Elsa, Oberleutnant Eberhard von 8

Ultsch, Hauptmann Fritz 15, 19

Wacker, Unteroffizier Paul **40**
Walburger, Unteroffizier Andreas **37**
Werfft, Gefreiter (later Hauptmann) Dr Peter 37, 110, 118, 120
Woldenga, Hauptmann (later Oberstleutnant) Bernhard **6**, 6, 7, 9, 11, 15, 40, 49, **1**(52, 123), **74**, 81